possessions

poems in american poetry

alan botsford

ISBN: 978-81-8253-930-3

First Edition: 2022
Rs. 400/-

Cyberwit.net
HIG 45 Kaushambi Kunj, Kalindipuram
Allahabad - 211011 (U.P.) India
http://www.cyberwit.net
Tel: +(91) 9415091004
E-mail: info@cyberwit.net

Printed at Thomson Press (India) Limited.

What is it then between us?

– Walt Whitman

The notion that a poet should have a distinctive voice is essentially a romantic one, or perhaps a symptom of the bourgeois cult of the individual. Can a poet not channel VOICES, play with contradictory styles? I'm not made of just one thing; why should my poems be?

— James Knight

...a sequence, one voice running through many personalities, contrasts and repetitions.

— Robert Lowell

Possessing what we still were unpossessed by,

Possessed by what we now no more possessed.

—Robert Frost

Contents

Prologue

i The Reader

—after Munro Leaf's *The Story of Ferdinand*

i

Smelling the flowers just quietly
was Ferdinand, childhood bull
of my early reading days, lulling
in the shade of forgetfulness
hours of hot afternoons lazily
gone by… What I
remember, buzzing
now in my mind's ear, and the
bookish pastures reappear, clear
as the days I wandered about in, on the clover-
scented trail of each new story read
while happily moving not an inch
out from under the tree
that spread its branches wide and far

into the world I would
come slowly to know.
O! It was the future as it made
a beeline for the
ground where I sat, that stung
me into every next step I had to take while
the branches of the tree kept keeping
pace with me—its roots
invisible yet always carrying
me past what my eye could

see, to this horizoned tree I still
lie under, smelling the
flowers, just quietly, thinking…

ii

…This boomy day
I pray will last
to bind the night
like a bonnet fastened under
a baby's downey chin
and wrap us in communal soft arms
the way one's birthplace remembered
of one's body believing
of one's soul, follows
us back, colors us black,
humble, lowborn, of the lowland
lovesick for you like a lovebird
unabashed, abdicating all thrones & titles
to abide our sojourn, our eye
abeam with the kelson
by which this ship—deep in its craft—abides
aboriginally, we mates
of May… our A-, B-, and C- horizons
rudiment, like a yawn,
and as contagious, a buttery biology
of hovering, floating
past scorn and shuddering fear to abet
no aberrant (aboral?), but
this alloying—with or without allusions—
to the all-or-nothing alliance
of our allotted daze,
amazed to be here (if here be allowable)

in this patch of knotgrass—this clover
of lovers' scent and butter-cupped alleluia beard lighting our chins!

iii

...In this way, growing
conscious of my unconscious I grew.

I grew to new lengths and heights
above and beyond expectations.

I grew the hands and feet and legs and arms
and torso and neck and head and back and shoulders

all from a seed inside me growing.
I grew the nose and mouth and ears and eyes I used

to plant myself deep in the soil of my soul.
I grew and grew until

I could grow no more...
and grew tired...and settled down...

and made growing a memory
I keep inside my sacred chest

that beats and throbs and grows
somewhere I know not where,

that goes somewhere
I know not where.

ii Uroboros to Narcissus

All this time I've been eating
my own tale, with no beginning
and no end. Yet how can I sing
without somebody or other hearing
my story, not to offer understanding
so much as a reason for telling
it to begin with. A life bordering
on death, it turns out, is one containing
the negation of itself, and brings
into the fold a new reason for being:
birth or liberation of those forms taking
shape in the very act, as now, of imagining
who we are or can be, pressing
the human mind to hear its own singing.

iii The Topological Imagination

—after Angus Fletcher

Close the book on identity and open
the filter of the motion picture
through which we view our world
and you will see, to start with,
boundary crossings that defy description
and test the imaginative capacities
of, yes, civilization. For on such making
the space-time continuum we inhabit
variably exists. Thought's perimeters
are forever changing in response to
circumstances the mind finds itself in—
History by any other name. Vico's cycles
pertain no less than Ovid's metamorphoses
to ascertain the height and breadth of the
mythic mind. Objects accrue there,
to be sure, as psychic terrain bounded
by a flow continuous as it is fluid.
It is in this flow I locate, such as it is, the I.

iv Black Hole

Shopping for hope? Death
repeats itself (not history) over
and over again to make us feel
alive. Make no mistake, however.
The dead, in being taken away from us, celebrate
their departure into air, earth, water, fire
—the fire of dissolution, the fire of annihilation,
the fire of regeneration—with the zeal
unmatched by any save those who desire
the world they live in, turning
and turning on the wheel of loving
the pain till death do us
part, divining once again (by subliminal
motion) (and emotion) what rends
and tears the flesh
into spirit.

*

If death is a black hole we fall
into, imagine, being the stars
we are, coming back to life
in another galaxy far distant
from ours, where in surveilling
spacetime, the living can still
learn from us long-ago dead.

v American Voice: a primer

A cento

now first having read the book of myths
I step through the door full of curiosity, wondering
if you will make me (O Lord) thy spinning wheel complete...

now hearing your words (and not a word among them)
begin, ephebe, perceiving the idea
poem of the mind in the act of finding
(yes love set you going like a fat gold watch)

now traveling through the dark
of night-blooming jasmine
—a realm is here of masquing light
can you hear a quavering cry, a screech owl?

now diving into the wreck
swimming by night
passing through huddled and ugly walls
I can tell you, hearing the shrill leaves
this is a hard life you are living
living in the earth-deposits of our history

now Hatteras calling
now the lynching
now hanging from the beam
now a light going out in the forehead
now wanting to die
now a black man talks of reaping

then I saw what the calling was:
...river that must turn full after I stop dying...

now skimming lightly, wheeling still

turning slow

in memory of my feelings

now all the new thinking is about loss
all my shortcomings, in this year of grace

now lying in a hammock at William Duffy's farm in Pine Island,
Minnesota
sitting at night on the front porch
now in the waiting room
I heard or seemed to hear the chiding of the sea
Now after making love we hear footsteps
the spiders marching through the air
night covers the pond with its wing

now I am holding this turquoise
munching a plum
(amazing grace in the back country)
it's this crazy weather we've been having

now clouds gathering
the storm is sweeping o'er the land
somewhere someone is traveling furiously toward you
there is a little lightning in his eyes
think of the storm roaming the sky uneasily

now in the quiet of the rain of morning
wither, midst falling dew
an old man bending I come upon new faces
bobbing in the waters of the womb
now at the end of my suffering
now I have seen a lovely thing
a blessing in disguise
let us go then, you and I
nothing gold can stay

(Composed of first lines borrowed from well-known American poems of the 18th, 19th and 20th centuries.)

vi The hatred of poetry

—after Ben Lerner

There is no poem better
than the one *not* written,
especially by yours truly—
a poet by any other name.
But who dares to call herself
poet, in this or any age?
Poets, despised more than
misunderstood, can tell no
tales like the dead—which
is what one must be before
one's read. For my part
no poem, no matter how
good, is one I'm equal to.
Whatever I write, its light
will shine in the next life,
not in this one, if I'm lucky,
which stretches my life
across time and space
in persistent disregard of death,
which is the aim, after all,
of poetry, writing it or
reading it. Which brings us
to Whitman, our poet with
a capitol P, bard of immortality,
he of a 6th grade education
and a calling to representation
of modernity's Republic, who

wrote the road movie of his
mind's eye and took us all
along for the ride—to eternity
and back, having found (were
I him) my mate in an all You
that strips me of me and leaves
me with a you and we, a spell
his poetry performs, magic-
and music-wise, incomparably
fine, his common man's fanfare
resonating and reverberating
communally, as only we can
who perform our rite as well.

Part One

walt whitman and emily dickinson

i

It won't do to ask the poet who
he wants to be. You would do
better to ask to seal memory
in a tomb where there's room for
death and love side by side:
Emily's less is more in a big way,
while Walt's shapeshifting grace
led the race into America's heart
in the afterlife only they shared.
The past the poet presents us
with, far from withering on the vine,
rises from the ash all fathers know,
who would taste the future on
their tongues, before the birth cry
was a shout-out to heaven-can-wait.

*

Emily was content: I am Nobody. Who are you?
Walt was not. I celebrate myself, and sing myself.
And what I assume you shall assume.

His cosmic me saw what was free
and tried to say it simply: you are me!
In the garden of the lion, I thank you.
In the garden of the ant, I join you.
In the garden of my heart, I am you.

Walt Whitman was ready. He was smiled upon.

ii

Emily pried open surprise
and found wonderment there,
intensest pain to the brain's
coiled interest, led circular
out, by degrees, of the flame
she lived wholly in.

Walt's prize was a nation
new to itself, and bolder too,
of a future that hadn't been told
until writ by his making, imagined
true, sane, released, to you.

iii his sympathy

Uncle Walt,
charged with the protection
of our souls. Or self-chosen,
as the case may be.

*

Clinging passionately to his
country, he would not let go of
democracy's promise, still being
made good on by those who
won't, let us pray, let go of him.

He doesn't bail.
He refuses to fail.
He keeps alive
his dream
and stays on the trail
he calls the Open Road.

Mad aim?
No! no! Walk on by,
and as for protection from the harsh elements,
commending this grass to sit on.

But re-leaf the grass
a thousand times
and still, it would
sound a song of myself
for the ages,
step on it all we will.

He had to
chant the self
through himself.

Whitman
in our midst on a gut-level.

Not Who am I?
but Who am I to you?
am I nothing?
or could I be something
true
past present or future?
this the poet's view

in his song of myself,
this the clue
to his cosmic self's music.

*

Law: what is written in stone
Spontaneity: what is written in water
Sincerity: what is written in blood.
But binding all together, Whitman said, is love.

iv mad flight… revisited

Bold—Reckless— Dead.
Prudent—Peerless—Read.

v Emily's rebellion (her voice)

Languageless is not silence
dwelled in, nor without syntax
of its own, twisting cranial
assertions heavenward as earth
defies gravity, star-like,
felt acutely, interiorly
where pain subsides in waves
ridden as inbound tide.
I'll have taken the gift home
that plashed onto shore,
to gain fame of my muse,
tortured by grammar's fuse
into a lined, perplexing form
I'll have dug out of graves
before I've obeyed,

sounding through time,
my juried psyche,
outlaw of history
called Circumference,
sentenced by the glacial
movements of a heart realigned
to the rounding art
judged potent, free.

vi

Dickinson and Whitman are more than canvasses to put your experiences on.

It's true: nothing
is more conspicuous than an empty reception.

But if I were to stand beneath the Sistine Chapel ceiling
of their up-raised spirits trying to describe its effect on
me I would say: *Impossible to imagine, this grandeur.*

What do they do, my heroes,
besides keeping me on my toes
and in the throes
of worship?

They turn up…

vii Emily Dickinson

The muscle she flexed
was the brain she sexed
tuned to those texts

that had readers flummoxed,
perplexed and vexed,
which is how she hexed
no age she lived in, but beyond—
eternity annexed.

viii Emily's journey

It's leading to lunacy,
her poet's journey,
a 'Lunacy of Light'
driven by night
into things missed
before they were lost,
where no longer will sleep
stain reality,
sleep will
open reality,
hence Poetry—
absent the power to tell
the difference Heaven
makes in Hell.

ix

"When I state myself, as the representative of the verse, it does not mean me, but a supposed person."—E.D.

To forge a voice
none can hear except
through what others say
—those 'supposed persons'—
speaks of the soul, bodily,

in conflagration:
let the ashes be swept
away, as refuse,
for it's the wick,
sparked line by line,
that stays lit,
when not confined,
by what's before
it, to rise by
dint of flame, what,
belying, comes after.

Amherst Belle
forges a boon
for her benefactors...

Shards of the Mystery
pierce the Soul,
splintering lines of poetry
released as the Whole.

x Sleeper (after Whitman)

Deep in space,
outer or inner,
while time flies,
sleeper's the winner
of sighs.

What's overly familiar
wears a face,
like a liar
leaving a trace.

Titillating, yet untitled.
Scintillating, without kin.
Soul got flayed.
No, he got played.

xi Emily's—

(her voice)

Mine— to be excavated by
the I in my sky;
yours— to be like
a door to your psyche;
ours— to be spent
as coin of what's dreamt;
his— to go past
what's uppermost;
hers— to be rehearsed
in stages of last;
theirs— to be inherited
through a spirit
breathing for
the body at its core
that opens and shuts
as time permits
and space retrofits
according to
—here's a clue—
one's own wits:
in hell or heaven,
without exception,
that is the question.

xii walt whitman university

You want to go to school
but need a university?
Look around you.
There's your university.
There's your universe!
What more do you need?
Look no more. Enroll in life.
Walt Whitman never got past 6th grade.
In Walt Whitman University
everything & everybody
is your teacher!
You don't have to pay tuition.
For full details, read
the poems of These States!
That's a lifelong education, is it not?
From beginning to end, we're here to learn…
It's not a rehearsal
It's not a trial offer
It's not like anything
you've ever seen—
day after day,
everyone you meet—
either the body is immortal,
ashes to ashes
mingling in some
other form with other
bodies—manifesting
with other bodies
or
spirit is immortal—
his breath merges with ours

his memory merges with ours
his dreams merge with ours
It is so easy—everyone can do it!
There is no special background to do it
No special experience required
It's called being alive!
to pain
to doubt
to suffering
It's limited time only?
You can only get this (offer) through his poetry?
No!
Eventually we stop asking why?
We stop asking questions?
Walt Whitman in his poetry never stops asking questions
but he reminds us that questions are
worth asking…
and he has answers!
Like the Wizard of Oz—he's the guy
standing behind the curtain pulling all the levers
to make the smoke come out.

xiii Emily's (in)direction

Thought twisting from a brain
circumnavigates the globe again
in syntactical maneuvers—
  she mans the fort of belief
assumption at a time, verse
victorious as the thief—
thought's riches carted off by train.

xiv another Walt poem

What bee stung you into the ring, Walt, into that arena
 cleared and amorous of grass, growing & growing?
What being (besides human) took you by the hand, O Poet,
 and raised the work to form?
What bullish horn gouged a hole in the side of death's shadow
 and made a show of desire torn free, newly born?
What spear-header led your campaign and rallied the forces
 of your embodied fullness, to that victory beyond words,
 beyond angels converting their trumpets of gold into
 the music of earthly spheres?
What happy fault, Walt, did you believe in that would never,
 O not ever leave you, that you could not bear losing
 yet that you lost again & again to find you,
 in your loss turned into the founder
 of what in others would be a 'real find'?
No need now to struggle with the meanness of lesser minds
 (or are they greater minds, Walt?) as long as the vein you
mined stays open for business, its shares given away
 now here, now there …the giver out of sight
 but not— never, o never— out of Mind.
What perils for the pearl's price would you risk, Walt,
 that would leave you stunned & messy,
 far from complete?
…Lost one, have you not had enough yet of supposed
 remedies & surprises that would… spread… you… out…

*

Gets to you,
communing with Walt?
The ghost

as host?
The ghost the exorcist
exorcises could be yours.

xv Emily's metamorphosis

Private life made tantalizingly public
draws you in, like a lit window
at night as you pass it by, wondering.
She'd bare her soul, daring the whole
picture to be seen, in a flash—ecstasy
across the liminal threshold, sung
in the throes of crisis, passion, death
she would outlive, split chrysalis
of a long-chambered heart in flight,
wings light-suffused, embodied Monarch.

xvi Walt on America's poetry of the future

What harbingers there be of literary
greatness revolves around the People,
no less august for being varied and various,
inclusive of all, exclusive of none, the fall
our language invites into disaster notwithstanding.
The war, I mean, crucial to These States, has
drawn battlelines of a different sort,
a requisite, carefully orchestrated music
of incoming storms. May it serve us well,
and tell of our greatness, as only
the ensemble elevated can.

xvii Emily's design

Who holds the key to a broken
lock, but the locksmith who,
when called, arrives punctually.
One proper turn and what opens is
more than a door that swings
in or out, but a shore between us
that you can be sure will never
be reached. Or is that breached?...

Ardent decider takes the hand
of chance and bestows a garland
of contingency on the world for
every poem written.
There she is, controlling nothing
so much as the moment that would
take her nowhere and everywhere,
hiding out in her father's shadow
from which she draws divine inspiration,
longing to lineate a life lived as
poetry, paginated as loves lost and
found, book-ended by the dare to
death to show itself for the absolute
negation of self it is, for her, and
rising to meet its challenge: This
she would design one flower at a
time, to be trespassed as in the first
Garden, and forested as a ward of
Nature, pure and indelible as God.

xviii Serpent (after Dickinson)

Most poets have a snake poem
up their sleeve, give them half a chance
and their snake is given leave
to dance from the margins of a page
to the center of the next new stage.
When a poet doesn't look up, though,
she stares down eyeball to eyeball
the sound of its sneaking around,
like an intravenous tube coursing with blood—
that arms-toting Rambo in limbo again,
pent up with the slo-guns of the rage
of Mars bearing his hearing until it lists
with listening, of fellowship of that ring
of fire prayed through daily, if not there
among men, then here in holy remembering,
vertigo-struck by the descent into a birth
without violence, that is the death of amen.

xix the cryptic messenger

For support she had Sue, her intellectual equal,
who savored the verses and epistles sent to her
by her sister-in-law next door, a tie steeped in honest
affection and deep passion which sustained the poet
in dark times. 'I'm so tired and desperately
lonely' are not phrases she would have written
to her beloved Sue, but words to that effect
could have been read all the same by her
unfailing muse, from the cryptic messenger,
'The New England Mystic,' 'The Eccentric Recluse.'

xx Dickinson after Bloom

The imagination, like the mind,
gets blown by the reality life
throws at it, non-stop, from
all angles, past present future
to open a plotless narrative
we didn't see coming from afar.
What encompasses us, in pursuit
of our fate without limit, is
what defines us, trembling on
edge of eventualities we have
no way of knowing otherwise,
so we slow the vision down
to a visionary extravagance
of letting sight behold itself
under the star of difference,
unnamed, but for a stopless sun
that time turns into appearance
and space, into a nihilistic pause.

xxi

Asking who is right is wrong,
I've learned, just as tasking sight
to carry the burden of appearances is
unsound. So round and round it goes,
the circles of claim, counterclaim moved
by the weight of a pendulum that
talks its way into a balancing act
between what's yours, ours, and theirs
at the borders of time and space.
A thriving commons
where we gather to mourn,

reminisce, pray. Is this
what Whitman meant when
he wrote, "And to die is different
from what any one supposed, and *luckier*."

xxii Whitman in old age

What is lost comes last
to my heart, to fasten
itself close, to hasten
the end, such as it is,
which I can see coming,
which I am going to
meet in the twilight,
in the dead of night,
alive in my bones
and alone, sufficient
for the journey ahead,
the body moribund,
the spirit curious,
outbound, eternal.

*

The holiness of 1892
when in that year Walt left this world
and joined the river of light,
his body uniting with the billions and billions
of departed souls known as the Dead,
becoming one
with that flow of energy
built up over centuries, over a millennia of time.

There for a reason.

xxiii

Shit.

Shit?

Shift.
Whitman's last words,
apparently. Although
there's some question
as to which word he
said. Maybe both.

*

Come find a place and
sit down, the grass says,
and you do.

xxiv Soulforge

"Dare you see a Soul *at the White Heat?*" – E.D.

(From the depths of soulforge she hammers out a poem, until
in the forge words fuse together effortlessly, as if by magic…)

(her voice)

i was thrown into the white heat, the tumult and trial,
the ferment and turmoil, the flurry and disorder.
i was convulsed by and floundered in
the shivering and shuddering,
i ebbed and flowed, i waxed and waned,

i pumped in the swinging and fluctuating
to quiver in the sway
and flit in the pulse.
i pitched and plunged, i bobbed and weaved,
i tossed and tumbled from pillar to post,
side to side, round and round, in and out, up and down,
until the ardor of the cheerful fire had me crackling,
thermally loose in the burning and fully alive in the blooming,
the blush of dawn, the glisten of night
gleaming and blazing in my blood,
gossamer and solid were the circuits of my heart.

xxv *I aggregate myself*

Poet in an apt
situation, paradigm-shifting
via a new zeitgeist
in myriad contexts
evolving and evil-looting
towards what exactly…?
Exactly! What is it
if it's not to be discovered en route,
whatever suits
the situation you're in?
Able to get further and further
inside the experience
of the tree
whose roots and branches
permeate and fill the
world we live and love and die in.
It's a mind-bending,
imagination-stretching,
heart-expanding journey

to the center of the
Earth we all inhabit
together: where the present
is past the future for
the moment and music of time.
Advancing far, far into
freedom's realm in harmony
with mortality and immortality both—
this is Earth's song, by my oath!
...So long!...
Your soulmate,
Walt.

P.S. And remember,
you're not at fault; you're genuine,
you're the salt of the earth we call
home. Keep cooking up the raw data—
Till later!

xxvi

What is the grass...
As grass grows, glows grace.

herman melville

At sixteen I dived into your spermic effluence
and wore the raiment 'nineteenth-century' as my own
not in lockstep but in sympathy, Ishmael I called
myself, long before the Song…

i

His line of sight took him far
out to sea where the ship of state
riding the waves of (in)humanity
follows the monstrous captain of
vengeance and violence, a quandary
inherited by so many generations
on its heels, that now we stand
for nothing less than the haunting
of a ghost republic whose sails
we see in the distance, history
by any other name, a mirage
we keep returning to as some hope
clung to, for a tale of survival
we cannot live without. His White
Whale being the male prerogative
taking us down into the maelstrom
of a futureless present, while the past
festers on, one leg at a time, to hold
a funeral rite for the Easter
that never comes, the West
he saw was going fast
nailed to the mast of Power

run amok, a shell roaming
the bottom of a succumbed to ocean
fathomless not as mystery
but as a story clamoring to be told—

Beware totality,
lest it total you.
Beware wholeness,
lest it put a hole in you,
or drop you down a hole.
Beware transcendence,
lest it drive you round
the bend.
Beware movements,
lest they forestall
the moment.
Beware brooding,
lest you keep rooting
for the transcendent whole
totality you're not, of
social relations we are.

ii

In Melville, straight face
to face with Dick himself,
a giant of a fish story
waiting to get heard.

I'm not good at swimming
if you hadn't known
But I'm good at mapping
the unknown.

It's his
fish story—
The one that got away…

No, it's a
shaggy dog story.
Some of it is true,
most of it isn't.

His 'here' thrills our 'there'
with music of a love up and coming
through the fog of war, misery
and daily devastation.

Holy is his head, and wide his art.
The body of his work will spread
its message to the heart.
I'm not grumbling. What
you see, he says, is what
you get—and it ain't
some tall tale, nor
a whale of a story.
A school of minnows in
the wake of the
shark is more like it.
He knows the world's a dark
shadow that no arc, narrative
or otherwise, can outsail.

… We may have a story to tell,
but he has a story to live….

The belly of the whale is
not a place but a state of mind.

Don't let that fish get away.

He's been swallowed by the
whale himself, Jonah has.

The deeps he
sleeps in to
write his poetry!
A pioneer of
being swallowed whole
by his whale
of a story!
Out he comes
fresh but poor,
with newfound freedoms
of creative lore.

He's reeling in the fish
that nobody wants to catch.

To get out of the slough, slough off your old skin.
It takes guts, gutting the fish your mind has caught.
Do you have the guts to be crazy when you need to be?
If family's everything, then everything's family.

My fish in the sea, I fear,
are going to be depleted.

. . . .

Yes, the paranoid in search of a plotline
is the fish story of the ages—the one
that keeps getting away… But far be

it for me to say what species of fish
and how big it was, for I looked into
its eyes and was spellbound long
enough for it to squirm free from my
outstretched hands. Now all that's
left of it rises in my dreams out of
the river I've taken to visiting on
a moment's notice. There the gleam
in its eye, with the sun warming
its gills and its fins rainbowing
from the water's surface it rose up
out of and will soon return to, ties
us together in our creatureliness.
And what he sees in my longing
of a glance I won't ask, yet wonder
which story of his I'll turn up in
when his school reconvenes and
stories are swapped over lunch
mid-day, before the moon sails
into view later in the night, when
I lay down on my bed and gaze
out the window, wondering…

iii

He ransacked the whaling imagination
and laid waste the religious imagination
and in tatters was the whole
lot of his career ever after,
unable again to duplicate its poetry,
unwilling to promulgate its prose,
until his fate was circumscribed by
a once free-wheeling ambition and

a now all-consuming, disguised monomania—
between which self-doubt reigned supreme.
The retreat from his own private civil wars
brought growing obscurity in late life,
greatness not hustled for but bargained for
all the same, in (his) posterity's name.

edgar allan poe

i

Ardent from the start, by desertion
of the father, devotion of the mother,
and the disposition of his art, he rode
the maelstroms of his lonely, cerebral
imagination, detailing its darknesses,
its poverties fallen back upon, countless
departures grasped by the rhythms
of sentences heard, swaying to and fro
between body and soul, day and night,
speech and silence, a tale of woe
lived in reveries of the written word.

ii *The Raven* as the crow

crow before crown.
dough before dawn.

*

Crow rising.

*

Crows come out
cawing.

*

(In escrow
the treasure
of now
for the big show
of then.)

*

Them crows, big
and smart, one doesn't
want to mess with.

*

These crows you know,
like you know your dreams
and nightmares.

*

The crows bounding from rooftop
to treetop cast black shadows

*

The crow hops
on the rooftop,
pecking at a
persimmon he's put
in the drain spout

*

The guttural caw
issues the new law:
all that's left
make the most of.
So he does, turning right
on schedule to see the crow
looking down at him above
yet another vehicle parked in
the city he's come to occupy
just in time, that space opening
on a fall day absent colors
he would mix by a palette
shared the world over, creation's
cry against the walls closing
in with accelerating speed, ice
by any other name, to affix blame
for this or that transgression all
have made a home in, for justice
appeased, which space shrinks year
by year into his century's flowing maw
hooked by gravity's empirical claw.

*

The wise man said, Play dead.
And we're inclined to agree.
It's no novelty act we bring
but a fact for fact
round the clock show.
Welcome to it, crow,
caw all you will…

*

Crow's on the rooftop
I can't see him.
Crow's on the rooftop
I can hear him…

*

Hell-lipped into silence mouthfuls at a time,
days and days passing without a word.
What waiting brings is more waiting.
The mind is unstirred. Pick-hoed in the gullies.
Now nobody talks, nobody walks
but the crow on the rooftop, hopping
and skipping under a winter sun, is another
mouth outrun…

*

you come
down here
to mirror what's
up
lots of birds today,
every which way
songs behind and in
front of me, indoor
songs and outdoor songs
heard
not on the run but on
foot nonetheless, ever so and
so like a
wish already flown
away, like the crow saying,

"Hey, wait
for me!"
in a sky full today
of other
crows.

*

Suddenly a crow caws three times.

*

Caw, caw
Let the crows caw
but answer their call.

*

No mid-wifery, no poetry puffery
No witchery, no wizardry
No history, no mystery
No sexery, no hexery
No buffoonery, no trickery
No goddessery, no goddery
Just this present moment in the belly of the beast:
about your past life I can tell you nothing
except what will be your future is contained in it
the way a crow's cawing contains the crow.

*

While the crows loudly declaim
their territoriality, the butterfly

flutters by
on wings miniscule to the sky.

*

The crows will know, if you try to show and tell.

*

Harassing the hawk
are the crows
in the sky,
who know
how.

*

I'll caw you,
said the crow.
But don't
believe a word
it says.

*

The crow knows to flee
at the approach of me,
the way the edge, in
being approached, recedes.

iii

He chewed off faces.
Nothing wrong with that
in his book of horrors.

The debaucher finds well
in his strength
while, unmasked, he contorts
his talent to stay
alive, exposed to the elements
of slander and neglect.
What lay beneath, lay
between the lines of
his stories, never reaching
the bottom of a bottomless
well of gruesome terrors.

*

The organism opens and closes
in the house of its pain.
The leaves turn and return
under the drops of more than rain.
The crow tells its tale
blacker than its stain.
The door will not open
to just anyone—
crossing the heart,
in death
is hope again.

*

Am I a crow?
(Don't I know.)
Am I a hawk?
(I won't talk.)
Am I a sparrow?
(   )

Too many crows have known
my secret.
I've been cawed to death.

Crow, and plenty of it,
to eat and savor
will add flavor
for dishes to come.
Home, as the crow flies,
is straight ahead in circles.
Listen. Listen. Listen.

*

He crows
just be-caws
he knows how.
But a swan he is,
a songster
taking a dive.
Don't follow him
there or you
won't come back.

*

Yes, these crows you know,
like you know your dreams
and nightmares…

*

Crows crowded in no
darkness but their own.

*

They were in my dreams
…trying to dream me!

*

The swagger of an American
gives me the heebie-jeebies,
for true genius is of a different
ilk than the rest of us.
But his writing clarifies
the fog for me. The mountain mist
it becomes, and the view past it is
stupendous. Yes, Poe has a leak in a
disturbed mind, it can't be denied,
but his is a genius of a different order
—one that also marks the trail to horror
and madness. Who can follow where
he leads, with all the risks involved.

…Like crows' eyes
peering out of the darkness…

edgar lee masters

(his voice)

Spoon River talks in my sleep.
Spoon River is my soul to keep…
Anywhere is better than here,
was the lie I told, words mere
shadows of the truth I knew,
for a freshening of the view
I would give, were my vision
whole, and without sub-divisions.
Now the City darkens to my
familiar neighborhood, one I
settle in, in a neighborly fashion,
where each soul I meet, each love
arrayed, would sooner cash in
on the hereafter high above
than what lies down below—
that rivery, pulsating flow
lit by the darkness I judged
to be the world, acknowledged
in a language deep and changed,
like so many tombstones
re-arranged.

stephen crane

— after *'A man saw a ball of gold in the sky'*

Accomplishments past all honor
are past accomplishment only
in the night, viewed in passing,
where the thrust of its moment
won't hold. But where it holds,
the singing starts, the swinging
to and fro, the swaying as of art
to the beat of the ages beyond
all time save the time you cannot
see—because there is no
time to see—yourself in, the moment
that, in spite of yourself, stops, takes
its measure and is accomplished, turning gold
which today we, yes, we have had
in *his* dance a chance to see.

gertrude stein

(her voice)

Einstein asked: What did you want to be
when you were growing up?
Myself, answered Picasso.
The two old icons perfectly matched
in wit, warmth and repartee.

*

If it's never too late
for the future,
it's never too early
for the past.
While the present
is always on time.
Don't tread on me, tradition,
nor betray me. Stay
near the edge and woo
the abyss with me, one word at a time.

*

Some words come to my mind
like leaves on a pond's surface, then I add to it.

*

Well, you know, the poet frees
the things he looks at,

doesn't try to enslave them
in a pre-conceived, ego-driven
frame.

To attain that magnitude of
vision is no small feat.

*

Just pluck the apple
from the tree and see
the serpent's tale that follows.
It goes on and on forever.

*

Things we come out of:
a bubble, a shell, a trance,
a nightmare, a house, a womb, a tunnel…

*

United, or untied: you choose.

*

One who knows, undergoes.
One who undergoes, knows.

*

Nobody owns
the unknown.

*

Reason and logic compel by reason and logic.
The unconscious compels by laws of the universe.

*

Taste is a test of how freedom expresses itself,
each according to his own.

*

The scandal brewing between my legs,
the future in my crosshairs,
anonymous be thy wares for now,
and contemplate the moonlit
back-end of a whole
new way of
seeing
the sun-drenched artifacts
of time
that say—I couldn't find
the words but the words
found me
wanting
what I couldn't have
done without
you.

robert frost

i portrait of the poet

Simple or complex,
he's quite a rex.
Fire on ice
or ice on fire.

ii

Led by pleasures principally poetic
which he aimed for and soaked himself in,
he presided over a life which fed his spirit
to the end. What tragedies he met along
the way led to his deepening "lover's quarrel
with the world," testing his own endurance
in the face of darknesses he found within
and without, and altering the landscapes
he braved—the unknown by any other name.
An Odysseus he was not, however, yet as a San Franciscan
a stranger all the same, in a strange land, New England,
in whose soil was sown the seeds of poems
which grew, past fear, into a forest he could
roam at will, a boy's, while the man toiled.

iii Frost on Wordsworth

It seems they want a conversation
where I want a deposition, a call
to judgment, to wrongs made right

in the face of cruel indifference.
They would converse with night?
We agree, then, on the wherewithal
required to overcome the silence
at the root of things, before a seed sings.

iv

Fire or ice,
both are nice
ways of desire
to be felt,
depending on
the hand one's dealt.
But rise or fall,
consummation is all.

v

Like a burly cop, the pressure
sits atop your body, insistent
and ready to cuff you, haul
you off to yesterday, stuck
inside there to do your time
in the space of a poem. He knew
his news would travel, though,
which was more than good enough
for him, counting on today for tomorrow
outright, as the manly fate he'd welcome,
court even, poet becoming his myth.

vi

Frost was not
kind. His bracing enough
strength was in using his mind.

Heart-mender, or wall-mender?
Robert had Frost for veins…
Mend yourself without him. Back through the purifying
fire…

wallace stevens

Concurrently flowed the dream in
reality of him who rode the language
bare backed between the evergreens
into the grove where he woke, the snow
having fallen lightly behind his eyelids
in a wintry sky, grey for being comfortless
and sad, and February bound. Thus sun-
haunted, he prayed in litanies of dazzlement
to no god but his own, elemental lion
between the floorboards of the house of man.

william carlos williams

He aspired to the majesties America
made him pay for, the sick rot he rose
up from part and parcel of his vision
generous to a fault, embittered as well,
earth-bound he would remain, the heights
off-limits to one such as he, who made
poetry out of his pact with the New World
shores he stayed on to his dying day,
while Pound, Eliot & H.D. expatriated
to the Old World, its mythic mind they
would re-absorb while he stayed in things,
rooted in the familiar streets and houses
that inhabited his imagination note by
note, a music of local spheres, American
speech by any other name, philosopher
of the plum and the wheelbarrow, his teeth
cut on births and deaths he, as physician,
daily witnessed in neighborhoods of the real,
letting the pure products of America have
their say, upon which so much depends.

*

'No ideas but in things'?
There are the ten thousand things
that no ideas can equal; yet
with ideas the things themselves
travel far and wide into the world.
Thank god for ideas.

ezra pound

i

He was in the debris
of what once was…
He was in the ruins
of what has been…
He was even in the wreckage
of what might have been
And still he
gave his all—
Come then
Calm down
For it's dawn
on light feet
who won't come again
like today,
like today.

ii — after *Personae*

The I-less wonder selves
up and down the streets of
the Unreal City, finding
what he looks for by closing
his eyes and dreaming up
the sky with all its stars in
full swing. Time settles
debts in his absence and
when he returns, the space

he occupies reveals hours
he didn't know he'd lost,
the days unwinding, oscillating
between who he was and who
he will be, minus
the instantaneous death
he takes along with him
for the ride.

*

Uncle Ez hints
by what he says, of
madness divine, line
by line one can't toe
without, well, risking
losing one's mind.

(That which spans
the centuries in your head,
Ezra-inspired despite the pounding
received, the tempering years
of aftermath, years of attrition,
years of disdain and the pain
of isolation, you enter,
crossing the threshold to meet
Oz, he behind the curtain
of ash.)

iii — after Daniel Swift's *The Bughouse: The Poetry, Politics, and Madness of Ezra Pound*

Inside D.C.'s St. Liz the microscopic giant
fed on the apertures of grief and
unreason, pallid in no gown made
of hope. He twisted the bars so as
to make life a reminiscence, his
muse bartered for daily. Nobody
who visited saw the man whole.
He parted from his personality
and let the stars thickening in the sky
turn a gutted, earth-ridden vision of
History he could inhabit, which took
him to the outermost mysteries and
back again poem by poem, cantos
sung to the accompaniment of selves
radioed and foreign who,
by speaking, would change the world,
though Amurika would have to do,
once read and passed through.

*

Have you pound it out yet, wit man?
Dante is daunting but Pound needs expounding.

The Poundian pencil crevicing the page
for less is more in a true war of words
where poet-warriors age a sentence
at a time and at a rhyme's notice
paddling link-by-link across Seven Seas
that sailors sing of or try to appease
lest they drown in bloody ink.

iv

Pound played at being poet maudit
and made an impact on the poetry
world still being felt all these years
later, but over-sized ambition for
the poet in society finally did him in.
The dream, however, while it lasted
fed a generation of poets who aspired
with him, to 'make it new.' This was
in part his gift, but the polis he sought
to create was bigger, as were his aims.

*

Literature is news that stays news, he said.
But (as we learn from his life)
what if literature is news
...that stays the noose?

Upon leaving America's shores for good he gave
a (fascist) salute. ...Or was it
upon landing back on Italy's shores?

Yes, Pound became an angry
dead white man long before he died.

But... the stars are looking down
and (for some) he's one of them.

marianne moore

i (her voice)

One will have turned
oneself into a great
poet by the end
beginning over and
over again, hair-pin
curves negotiated by
a vehicle of thought
workable for being
bound by the straight
lines of sight, sites
for poor eyes not,
the vision the thing
what cannot be said
otherwise, and one shall have
some testing, the velocity
of a thought and the arc
of its articulation.

ii

She dined on suppositions intrinsic
to freedom, hunger withdrawn
into a framework of philosophy
aesthetic in all dimensions save
one: the past having its say, too,
though who knew her father
would enter the collage of existence

as the one she never knew while
in her mother's grasp, if not bed,
her loveless life long, lovingly,
nothing replete, everything revised
till the Protestant was at home
in the world, citizen of the poem
in a lion's leap from the iridescent page
before she ate herself up, savage
undoing despite her seat at the table,
relished as a fable for our time.

robinson jeffers

(his voice)

the world rounding with love and hate
flattens into hell of the insensate
that, unremembering, lies in waiting,
the mouth of the monster salivating
jaws ready to open, moving, moving,
burning three thousand years (this fire
is no match…) felt of faults, who
was it started the healing, falling into feeling
the heat lurking below that the two-
footed mammal's shadow,
from looking up, came to know.

t.s. eliot

"April is the cruelest month, breeding
Lilacs out of the dead land, mixing
Memory and desire, stirring
Dull roots with spring rain."

i

They killed the lilacs, they who came, gardeners
paid to tend what he didn't have time for.
Thirst was theirs in the high summer heat
and to slake it he served them tea from the door
through which he over the years watched
the lilacs bloom, a bush burning with its own
desire for the light he did not, or would not,
overshadow. Outward the branches grew.
Inward the poet in him knew: They killed the lilacs
long before. Now I garden for free,
  singing—

My love is a tiger—it prowls the outer precincts
    of desire.
My love is a snake—it coils in and out of the coming
   and going
    of Being, together.
My love is a rat buried in the backyard one spring—
   from whose remains
a lilac bush has taken root, grown and
   blossomed on this page.

ii

Spring rain, the rich smell of it, April
mid-stride bursting at its seams, crocus-filled
scents infusing the grey afternoon with light
barely seen, felt as a touch on his skin
in pattering drops tap tap tap tap tap tap
and on the stones his feet scamper across,
umbrella-less, letters in hand, until he reaches
the porch and opens the door and disappears inside.

iii

When T.S. Eliot of
the tight canon
meets
Walt Whitman of
the loose canon…
look at the poetry
exploding around that poetry!

hart crane

i

“I see the warmth instilled in me
as blatant commodity
for which dour sea-change absolves
the lover’s taranquity.”

(This is an American archetype
flatlining between sun and earth
given to tidal reminders
of lunar resplendence.)

“I’m going to take a long walk;
I’m going to walk back from the center.”

(Then we have no hurry
to buy them, right?)

“I was alone and can’t think why
I would say come along with me.”

(Meanwhile heat survives in stone
like a spark hidden in perpetuity.)

ii

Arroway’s flint
besieges the air of
cleft distinctions—
now feathered, now flamed,

now further still— in
congress with ellipsis
there's no inhering to.

iii

He totally left behind
some deep realm of
the everyday, was more
a musician and rhythmitician
facing the dangers of
going too far into the music.
But that he ended
his own life
was most un-Whitman-like.

iv (his voice)

I would have called attention
(had I the attention span to last)
to the lasting frame poetry exerts
upon chaoses we traverse across
rapturous beams, moonlit trellises
manufactured, not made, for public
confession in a private language
no logic of metaphor could bridge,
but the space the times found me in
was where, momentarily, the parapets sang,
so I listened in shared abstraction
of desire, always a shore beyond,
and what words followed flowed
past the end like a lover leaping
into his beloved's arms, whole
and complete, in waves.

langston hughes

Langston's warmth heated every line
of his, even when the pose he wore froze
at the injustice of it all, Black man's cross
borne in a white man's land. But look
at his face, the smile worn, the steady gaze,
the dream deferred wholly for the sake
of time, his world of pain and musical design
not unlike the neck its fate's albatross.

stanley kunitz

(his voice)

The cold dark I dug down into
had buried treasures for me to unearth,
no wisdom, mind you, but death and rebirth
twisting like the knot of the tree
bark, and rising like sap as poetry,
wordless at times, that holds true
in silence, in a glance, a momentary
embrace. How do one's lines carry
weight, if not by the ancestors' stories
taking us there, which we channel
through us with a hint of scandal?
For we, by nature, would dismantle
the moment coming before, for the sake
of one true song in love's wake.
That, at least, is my only *Vita Nuova*,
Dante being a lasting supernova.

kenneth rexroth

i

The storied career
of a self-taught poet,
critic and anti-capitalist, anti-establishment
provocateur still carries weight, still
holds up a standard for younger,
would-be poets to follow.
The killers, both direct and indirect,
of the human imagination
is what he opposes
as he glories in the *agon* fearlessly.
But that the poet occupies a place between
god and human, where language situates him,
is a painful truth when connecting
to the poetry source.
But that's his cross. He must bear it.

This is our intuition
of nature, he says.
This is our afterlife
moment to moment.

ii (his voice)

It's drawn and quartered, the world is, into
pieces of a puzzle that won't fit no matter
how often you try. Spiritually speaking, you
die a thousand deaths just to gather
the essence into a line of poetry.

I've fought for the inside to remain a place
one could inhabit organically, not without
its violences, but intact, a solid landscape
one need not ever leave unless forever
in a loop from under to over and back again,
a hostile environment, then, only to those
who have left it permanently, and finding
no way back, lash out wherever and against
whomever they can, at unsuspecting targets
of simmering angers and boiling rages…

Let the secrets
speak for themselves
and the lies
speak for you.
Either way, the truth
will out in the end.

Cocks just crow
Mountains must grow

There are a hundred
inside miracles
a mountain shows you.

Not all Pleiades come
out in the sky, when
night-viewing is advised.

I stand for feeling
the consequence of loss.

w.h. auden

'I don't want to write it,
because I don't want to face it'
had no truck with him—
Auden's rebuttal to dying
was to live without lying,
told in the folds of his face
as his truth's saving grace,
unbearable were it not for
the lines he wrote, more
proof, if any were needed, of
his heart's deepest dives
into whatever rhymed with love—
world below, as above.

theodore roethke

i — after *The Lost Son*

Oozed by words, loosed by stars,
stone of patience, who are we?
The underworld underneath after
long silence will come through.
This vision we are waiting on.
Alone at sea. Look up, grainy flower,
look up. Immersed in dreams
you have come to life. Your day
is come. Night has taken you here
by ripple effect. Why how matters
is desire itself. Life without strife?
What a pair. Where else do we get words.
A well-circulated self, solid in sound.
Bloom and blossom fade into wetness.
Tick-tock, tick-tock…Be quick
up the mirror, laddered from falling,
unless by speech the center unfolds
into the present. To bone I held on,
and on. Let heart vouch as much.
Life be nimble, death be quick. I for eye,
truth for tooth, lip for whip.
Higher calling takes a humbler route.
In this perfect circle, green man,
build us a blessing from awe.

ii

He dives
into the mire
and rises on fire
in a dark time, sloughing
off the slime to stand,
yet a mind no higher than
the human choir.
(Under his bravado
lurked an abiding kindness
walking his comet
in the sky.)

iii — after Alan Seager's *The Glass House*

(early)

'Ted' rolled in the best company, mind-wise,
but had fantasies of power and success not
to be believed. His tendencies waylaid him
in hospital stays where he wrote some of his
poetry, always non-stop, the inspiration
not half his perspiration, bent on the coming
line—lifeline in his case, thrown to himself
to prevent drowning in his drama of the Self.
Where others came in was for playing out those
roles he tried on, and off to the races he'd go.
This was a mad genius who chanted the dance
in no trance but the body's, high stepping
with death to the outermost edge and back again.

(late)

The poet grew into a public man. But where
his flights would land him except for back there,
to the memory of childhood, to the father, a bear
of a man like himself, to language like prayer
uttered from the lips of the boy he'd share
his inner life with, rising over time, aware
from the depths, of the spirit split in two, the pair
reuniting in each new poem, breath turned air.

iv

The self unified, yes,
but as Roethke says,
Which I is I?

v

Roethke—now there's
a poet whose brand is
good. It factors growth.

But what about how he ended up?

Dead? We all end up
that way.

elizabeth bishop

i re: Robert Lowell, after *Correspondence*

(her voice)

We twirled the girl-and-boy thing
round and round, at first lightly,
then, without parsing, the anecdotes
accrued to a tidal wave of love and
attention we could not live without,
a pair of poets at opposite ends of
the spectrum if not, at times, the earth.
Fixed on Poetry's star which together
we had little time for gazing at, so
inured to its flickerings, that upon
hindsight we became each other's
star, for better (and worse, I fear,
in your case). But I have never met
anyone as fun as you, nor one as
given to astute punditry. Poetry,
it's true, constellated our lives around
it, to have a life by, always to the good.
The mishaps added up, but what
could we do? Holy the shrine of friendship
I prayed in, and out of fidelity there
grew a sea we could return to at whim
and will, never at each other's expense.
You in wave upon wave washed my soul,
if you could call it that, and restored
frayed nerves as we held each other tight

as the sea the shore, as only a shining
sun to a star dared, for which my gratitude
is, alas, too small a word.

ii Bishop in Key West

(her voice)

I retired into the sun enflaming
on the beaches of a poet's naming,
performing the rituals of woman becoming
what being human requires of loving,
the key, west or east, of the body thrumming
to the rhythm of waves incoming,
that I found would unlock the stunning
views I beheld while swimming
to shores vast and touching—
lines written for a daily homecoming
I spent nights envisioning,
heart unjaded in tides recurring
under the moonlight travelling
across the waters soundly breaking
on sands burnished, and always shifting.

iii

No character in extremis but
reticent, as she is often described,
(cerebral aneurysm took her away
for good), while in her poems she eludes
us, our version of who she was
dissolving in the minutiae of details
the great artist hides behind, her

eccentricities conflated with those
of Herbert and Hopkins, poets
affectionately read and studied
early on, before she wandered
in countries and languages far
from her native land, finally
landing back in Worcester, Mass.
where her mother was interred,
no victim of circumstance, pain
outweighed by (spiritual?) gain
in the gilded lines she wrote, what
in the end we imagine knowledge to be.

czeslaw milosz

Unsentimentally he sees the unicorn
prettily prancing in the grove, easing
past the tyrannical grip of brutal history,
signaling what should be, over what is.
Unsparingly he revisits the massacre
sites that space is comprised of, admitting
of each chilling, blood-curdling cry.
Yet the fairy story he tells speaks to no one
save he who never believed, or
had forgotten what a real unicorn looks like.

Part Two

william everson

(his voice)

American temperament drives
on two pistons—the frontiersman
and the aristocrat, two personas
to inspire Americanness. But
for the poet, the New Adam
reigns supreme, archetype
not of form but of energy,
the serpentine braiding itself
wherever it goes, deriving
its power from spontaneity
and improvisation, the structural
given way to the energetic flow.

delmore schwartz

He was a poet who took on all comers:
the clock, the walls, the streets, the City,
and beat them all to a pulp
fiction confessing his style, strutting
his stuff, mounting the heights, shooting
for the moon-cradled name in the bright
hunger of his life, music made for angels
brought down to earth in despair,
the god of hope betrayed by
'the withness of the body' without
slumber, without a dream to sustain him,
New York carnivore, hotel room loner,
emptied of heat, without a beat for his heart to walk
in the lumber and hustle of his song, barely
heard, yet wedded to the world in summer knowledge,
to the darkness beneath it all.

john berryman

i — after *Dream Songs*

Much has been made, more than I am.
There is no shade of consolation
speaking over the years one's lost.
It goes its way, and you yours, two paths
shared for the taking. Pile up, pile up,
mountain of my morals, where I climb
is no summit, no crevice conquered.
She beguiles with a song I hear, *Be*
at peace… No death save one, swathes
of which she leaves behind, voiced hologram
I'll enter as I please, to where the sword
holds no sway but that'd swiftly, triumphantly
upend what peace is for: the living
place to which they'd return, in a future
you've made your own, at long last.

ii — after Adam Kirsch's *The Wounded Surgeon*

This is why you won't scare easy:
it's all already dreadful, he thought.
And so it was, thunder and lightning-wise,
the breaking of spiritual bread aside.
But if being eaten is what the world taught
him was fate, a devouring no saint of Assisi
would wish for, let alone pray for, what ties
a man to wholeness, but hope's flimsy
thread to personality that has not died.

He would, he thought, agree to wake up
to its strangeness and punctuate it
for love of fame—though he'd come to hate it—
letting the chips fall wherever they will
neither above nor below fortune's wheel,
until from a bridge, diving, he'd finally look up.

robert lowell

i on reading Lowell

I felt frizzled, stale and small
when I took down a book of Robert Lowell.
In God do men honor meaning, retooled traditions
and exile allowable in the mania signed on for.
'Cal' told of the affliction his mania brought
upon himself and those he knew, and taught
the world the steep price paid for it was
one he could not *not* pay, so write about
the damage done he would, at all costs.
There is no smoking gun for the poet thus
afflicted. He won respite from illness
only in intermittent bouts, reckless seer
of history, of madness, of the blinding tear.
The parallel *polis* of his mind protrudes
in his poems imagined or recalled, mood
swings notwithstanding, to the tune
of a challenge, a danger, a lesson,
or a warning that we would
do well to heed, not later but soon—
to give each figure in the photograph
her living name, before in some taxicab
you meet your end. But until this soundtrack
ceases playing in my head, his zodiac
I'll keep reading, as a dead man's flow graph.

ii

His dolphin muse took depths at ease,
swum-through turbulence and clamorous seas.
He hatched violence in waves
to stalk the shore that memory saves.
What shifted the parlance into a dance
heated his steps, his breath breaking the trance.
When the other side became this close
to thoughts heard out of season, he rose
on rhyme as on a crow's black back
past the whiteness of the page, upwards
through cloud-banked sky, into space rent
with stars against a galaxied, milky void, for
a new place shorn of time, born the same
with what he knew to be history, this side of it
anyway, double-edged, inward, a manic dread.
To have made his mark, historically, while
between the lines lay lies against the disorder
rank in the muck and mire settled in, was all.

iii—after Kaye Redfield Jamison's *Robert Lowell: Setting the River on Fire*

Lithium angels in the sky, illusions
grander than the tongue on fire, float
across the alphabetical spheres into
words, one at a time, sentencing you
to pronouncements that shudder
with metabolic heat, heard confusions
you'd break free of, metaphors of note
to brine feelings made to re-order

the passage from highs to lows
that, god-willing, barely shows.

iv. arena: Robert Lowell

He would stand on the shore,
when far out to sea
you see him waving.

He would climb the ladder
and brush up his
speech with God:

Is this supposed to be twenty
thousand leagues under the sea?

And in a posture of defiance
he would lower the boom:

I'll not retrace my steps here
without calling down all
the angels in your kingdom
to stand by me, come what may,
and fight, not just to breathe,
not just to survive,
but to conquer my fears
of the unknown, of chaos,
of death.

v. history: Robert Lowell

In savage poetic truths he went to battle, time
and again, knocked down, brought close

to the precipice of his death, his madness
having stolen away grace, friendship, love
upon which his life, any life depends, and
each time he would return to the ramparts,
unforgiving of himself yet forgiving also,
of the fates, of the failings, of the farewell-
laden journey he was on, that would restore
his faith in who he was, in what America was,
or could be, as he learned to swim with
the tide-turning events of his time, history
by any other name which he, full of grace,
full of the love of others, honorably made.

vi. Lowell and Hardwick

—'Why not say what happened?'—

The carefree bonhomie he carefully mined
for baubles of the mind, heartlessly defined
as magpie's disposition hereby signed
to the poetic contract, that dotted line
crossed again and again until aligned
with the godlessness of the times,
save for the sanctity of historical fact
returned to, past art, as actuality's tact
now adhered to, or prayed to, fished
out of 'the grace of accuracy,' wished
for reality present until… it's published.

—after *The Dolphin Letters*

He evoked Keats, while she
turned to Hardy, the two writers

jousting for some redemption
in a literary contest of the age,
he the battle-scarred poet
undone by manic episodes
too numerous to count, she
the long-suffering wife willing to take him back and nurse
him, stark truths et al, memory-
haunted, letter-laden, but she the
victor, warm, confiding, whose
artful syntax and pacing shine on.

robert duncan

(his voice)

Hallowed these voices be
the primitive ear hears
in its prime, an all-told
never heard more than
a word now here, now there
going across some threshold
for movement musical
tuned to the outer-
most mind in depths we sound,
a recollection of spirits we are
possessed by and inhabit, as
believer of a bailiwick of non-
sense we wouldn't disavow, for
sense-making is over-
rated and logic lies, which
reasons out of faith,
out of love.

denise levertov

—after *The Poet in the World*

We dabble in what we would delight in
when we should open ourselves to the transforming effects of our sensuous apprehensions,
our inspired beings and becomings, our dance
with the unknown. We do not advance
but are set back by unreadiness of vision,
where the need to *make it new* fades
from our purview and we miss the chance
to name and praise *what is*, which degrades
the real to its facsimile, its faux possession.
The artist, if authentic, deepens our attention
to accord with, as WCW said, new conditions,
now bodily adapting to, now manifesting abundance.

jack gilbert

i (his voice)

Full of wit I try to sway you
to this way I'm on, of seeing
things as jewels they are
that'll boggle the governmental mind—
the breasts in red straps hanging like fruit,
the hand placed on a trembling leg.
What tears away at desire but desire
itself, no riddle solved, no wish
fulfilled. Here I am, half of me
says, the other half silent.
Matisse swore his blues, yellows and
greens to fidelity, and by grace
they help out. I swim in the rainy
season as the water pours down, the
tailspin I'm in making me dizzy for you.

ii

I suppose it is the feminine
that he has succored, that he
has sucked the marrow of,
his love
of the bone
of the moon
on loan from
the territory he passes through.

a.r. ammons

(his voice)

There was no place for me
in the whirlwind's center
without the death of me present
to the stillness within, watched
like clouds in the sky, by
the gaze of the lake water's
surface shimmering immortal
as a soul, or as a zero praised
no matter what it adds up to,
whirl forever inward turning
my compass for high traveling.

james merrill

The nobel Russian exiled poet who ached
to be like Wystan, *was* Wystan, he thought,
certain he was going mad, comes to mind
now as I leaf through the changing light
that JM channeled from the other side,
his poets et al mentoring him in seminars
that became the theater in his blood,
receding like footsteps to the grave,
each new day's transcript being
translated by a poetic touch he gilded
his age with, material of his he dug up
against all good sense, or as he says:
"And in the final analysis, who didn't
have at heart both a buried book and
a voice that said destroy it? How sensible had *we* been
to dig up this material of ours?"

Yes, he doused the spirit world
for voices overheard in sync
with crepuscular recombinants
and dipped-into ectoplasmic wavelengths
scuttling across logic's floor.
And now I wonder, had it remained on
sub-atomic levels unseen would he
have stayed in his body
and not been "imbued with otherness"
and forced to hear and see
that mental place called mystery
more real, almost, than the mercurial travesties
we know, alas, the heart's made of?

(Look into that abyss incarnate
and you'll see others' hate
embodied as a leaf
spreading its angelic wings
the way Christ's thief,
spreadeagled, still sings.)

Mere animal attention?
The apparently trivial matter
of fixed attention, fully
paid attention, attention
armed and active and all-seeing,
is not a trivial matter at all but
of great importance. But distraction
has its charms… For
the best attention, it turns out,
springs from distraction, the kind
that allows for eddies and flows
of inattention until ideas come
forth in creation's throes.
Like any other attendee, he came
to pay attention, to give himself
over to the act of creation that
asked of him his full attention. But
when you're sleeping, you're paying
a different kind of attention, when
you allow your mind to wander
you experience still another kind
of attention. We don't fall into
attention the way military ranks
now are required to do. If
attention, as the poet says, is
the beginning of devotion,
his lines are prayer.

robert creeley

(his voice)

Caritas places my eye to a fixed
position. *Eros* has the other
roving. In tandem, *agape* fills
my field of vision, the summit
reached, that I never thought
to go. She beckons, but I am
slow on the uptake. We aver
to the slope where I slip and
slide, hoping a foothold will
do the trick, for now, *philia*
by any other means.

galway kinnell

i

Family grew into formidable
forms he turned them into,
a maker following his
imperative; they
grew long against the
short sentences they took
shape in, they grew real
against the artifice
he made them fodder for.
They grew into a story
heard at the end of day,
gone into their telling
a detail at a time, until
the end rose up and found
the secret of its beginning.

ii on his passing

The senior scene would
fix it as an expression
of urgent devotion, a scene
of gentle devotion, not
murder. They would ask
how it ever got this far, the
landing on the moon and
the bombing of an innocent
land and its people. They

would patronize his poems
with a slicked-back gratitude
like his hair. They would say,
Keep walking! to the gawkers
who stop and stare at the bloody
wreckage of our life of the 20th
century. But they would add that
Mr. Galway Kinnell did his best
and did more than most to capture
the horrors, in words and images,
in the poems he wrote. They
would say he deserved better,
or more, than what he got—
(his obit and public send-off
in an impatient tone of voice).
He rocked us, though, and
we would be remiss not to say
how much we loved him for it.
Anything holding him down
he'd now let go of.
R.I.P. Galway Kinnell.

w.s. merwin

i — after *The Shadow of Sirius*

(his voice)

The spells of what is
written can come
undone at a moment's notice

The sound of voices
I never heard
before I went to sleep
can be listened to
in silence

A song I once sang
can rise in the dark
again, where I have not forgotten
the names, the remains
of which are the memory
of stars

But O nothing I know of has a lock
on luck like lack
looked at through
the lucent heart

ii the strangeness

(his voice)

it takes you suddenly
announcing there are no accidents.
where you go now is up
for grabs.
you've left behind the
familiar, now the horizon
seizes its chance.
the woods have their
way with you,
the path penetrates
deeper.
all eyes from behind the veil
of darkness are
focusing on a point
you cannot make out,
as the white dogs of night
gnash their teeth,
as the light in the distance
quivers, and the
shiver you feel sets
you on your way at last.
children walk the street
where you once belonged.
she who wanders
the years in a shroud,
unrecognizable, dogs
your steps.
beneath the canopies
of separation you
seek refuge, but
you won't be there for long.
the spaces you will cross
no pain will ever close

up again. the green
leaves waver in
the wind, and suddenly
the guide beside you
matching your every
step, shudders in uncertainty,
as you light out now
alone,
making for
the roar, the roar
inside the mirror

iii

There's nothing there but air
and a voice to go with it,
Merwin's infallible judgments
hovering god-like for the human
being broken into pieces, into light.

iv (his voice)

If Poetry's success is, by nature, posthumous,
I was ready to run with God all the way to Heaven,
until I remembered Heaven was down here on Earth.
Heaven, it's true, has held me homeward all my life
but friendship, our love for one another, allows
the seeds of time to grow farther than death.
Or that is my faith, such as it is, though espouse
it I won't, the rule being let the written word
speak plainly on the page in its own light,
sun-splintering darkness that shadows fold
into images born and given breath.

james wright

(his voice)

I love openly
the things I've lost
to the way things are
leaving as I speak
a language I've found
able to keep me where
I wouldn't be otherwise,
words that unveil their
riches, their abundance
all I ever needed for
this journey through
the world I learn by heart,
myself my home
soonest to be gone,
light, without night,
truly hell on earth.

maya angelou

(her voice)

I know what
history teaches, how
things are not
what they seem,
a treasure stolen,
a democracy negated,
a heart embalmed,
a sorry state
of We the people
squeezing others dry.
Yes, we know why
the caged bird
can't fly.

I am sick
of losing the thread
out of the labyrinth.
Let me be my own reward.

philip levine

"I'm an American,/ even before I was fourteen I knew I would have/ to create myself."

(his voice)

Staying here is not an option
to be considered without clear
markers of where the there is,
so here I go, delineating light's
return in the darkness I love,
blessing imagination along the way,
I— for whom the name 'American'
rumbles past like an airplane
you can't see moving across
a cloudy sky— yes, I hereby declare
creation is not an escape anywhere.

anne sexton

i (her voice)

My speech acts to further the dance
not at a distance. Not one-liners, or three,
that patter indulged in dismally.
Not quips to undermine pallid rivals
shuffling off-stage. For the age has a rhythm
all its own, a nervous system ineluctably coming
to be. Or not. Coffin it up.
Are you down with it? Are you found by it? Or are you
bound for it, stoic? Does the agon, strangely stirring,
lack nerve again? Or does the prologue
dog the cat out of the bag?

ii

Everybody's got their
own metamusic.
I'm not talking about
the songs. I'm talking
about their meanings.

Our poets & philosophers?
Heidegger was a Nazi.
Pound a fascist.
Eliot an anti-Semite.

I want you to see
the death of Europe

in me
the way Anne Sexton saw,
and Sylvia Plath,
and Emily.
It was the rage to order
succumbed to,
as if the sea
could be
ordered.
It was the sun
that would not die
in order to die
in its light.
It was the mind-destroying
page that would not speak
into the ear
the sound it needed
to hear.
It was the dust
in their time
that would not
settle.
And what to leave out
leaving silence
in its place.

john hollander

i —on a poem of his

Listening to Mozart while reading a sonnet
makes more sense than trying to forget
the old forms, or so sayeth the wise poet,
now gone, who lingered long in the song
of love to catch its music, not once and
for all but in the moment, his, memory-
laden and sublime, his fourteen-year-old
self self-consciously in love with she who
made reaching sixteen a matter of wisdom
deferred, until the older ways were
outstripped, and the new confessed its
embarrassment at the riches the years bring
to light late in life, follies notwithstanding.

ii (his voice)

The times have floated free of memory
space gives no sign of forgetting, day
by day, where even the dead try to delay
their reckoning, now and forever, to see
what they missed in living their lives
the way they did, grateful for how night
comforted them in their loneliness, not
of terror in the face of what never arrives,
but of what tunnels toward the end, in light.

adrienne rich

Her news stayed news
on the cusp of truth,
a change of world with
the female myths that use
up reflections of an eye.
There is no greater cry
more restless and miserable
than what she made believable:
woman enraged, freedom hard-won,
no mere prospect under the sun.

Part Three

derek walcott

i.m. 1930-2017

i

The poetic canvas attacked by the painter's brush
absorbs the blows, tainted by historical laws
obeyed in the arboreal pastures of memory
laid down in rows, as if these lines could flush
out the birds, etc. living there, for the eye to see
what branches hide from view, a deep privacy
not to be invaded, one that fed the gift of prophecy
he practices on the shoreline now, the fanned sea
he skims with a visionary glance which draws
us into the frame, left, right, centerless as sky
burning red with sun-dappled hues that rely
on our conscience, no prodigal, to welcome
boundaries kept intact, feral outlines of home.

ii on learning of his passing

We walk this earth, the span
of years a bridge we cross
step by step, to bend and spar
with the elements, bear loss
whose heaviness pulls us
where we need to go, not far
as destinations go, but spun
from the cloth of days
as nights rehearse in dreams

the journey's end, elsewhere
than one had supposed,
Heaven knows, for a gleaming star
above, the one that chose
you and led you here, goes
by gravity's arc downstream
to a wider river of light
you did not foresee, a glint
in your eye, a fingerprint
left on the page turned
of a book you will not read
without your being burned
in the chilling fires of the dead,
for whom space and time
have turned a dark matter,
through us entwined,
and all I can do is mutter.

peter everwine

—on a poem of his

(his voice)

I welcome the moment of remembering
like the soulmate it becomes, so I sing
of happiness it brings, the dissolving
into stillness to get a better view, hoping
the day won't disappear forever, as I
know I will, when my time comes, dry
the wine I've sipped, now easing my way
into the darkness, praying for another day.

harold bloom

i.m. 1930-2019

on his passing

the sad eyes, drooping
the music of the west, looping
in all directions save one,
in the grave settling
as sad notes on history
buffeting the eternal songs
composed by the mystery
of what he called sublime—
that sorrowful turned joyous
under cover of reading,
that influential journey of
the mind wandering through
the pages of night, presences
embraced in an *agon*
meant to overthrow
what it glories in, true
shapes love has borne
before the *clinamen*
back to the dawning
imagination, creator's wellspring
of words at the root of the tree,
the promise of poetry
of which he, singing,
still, is honoree

Heat rends the fabric
of night from within,
a light of prismic colors
we can't get any more perfect.

*

We partake of the critic's capacious
mind in hopes of, however contingently,
duplicating it down to its deepest paradoxes
and contradictions. To inhabit it,
capaciousness, after all is transportive.

jerome rothenberg

—Inspired by a talk given by the poet in Kyoto, June 3, 2010

(During his talk Mr. Rothenberg said, vis-à-vis leaving some poets out of his anthologies, "Anyone who takes the risk of living the life of poetry deserves the utmost consideration." He also said that in his writing he tries to stress the connection between poets and shamans but was quick to add he doesn't see himself as a shaman.)

(his voice)

Please don't be
scared of me.
The tears I've shed
have gone to my head:
Jewish are my people
even if they were sheeple.
I've got a story
to tell a mile long
and a millennium wide.
Lend an ear
and you'll know fear.
It's true for me
but not for you
it was my family
who went to the ovens.

History is where
the past goes to die.

We went there
long, long ago.
I'm already eighty
and feel weighty
from the stories
over the years
I've heard tell.
No new ones
enter these ears.

So, all I have to say
is: Don't be tame, sheeple,
  don't be tame
Look what happened to the Jews.
Don't be tame, sheeple,
  don't be tame
The Blacks, they sang the blues.
Don't be tame, sheeple,
  don't be tame.
Of your freedoms, human
  and beloved,
hear the news.
Don't be tame, sheeple,
  don't be tame
In the face of harsh realities,
  remember these views:
'I have bought & bought
  when I should
  have fought & fought.'
'Have some balls
  to have some fun.'

Me, I'm like kelp.
I don't need any help
floating & flowing
with the tides.
Just leave me be,
the days I don't
seize, I cherish.
My god, world, what
have you done?
Not I can come to the rescue,
all I can say or do
is: No need to line up
for what you already have!

Yes, I am the mistake that thrives!
Don't cross me out!
Don't be tame, sheeple,
don't be tame
Go out & have some fun!
What's up next
is anybody's guess.
Give it your yes.
Dry thesis will pave your road
but in this realm what's needed
is wetness to bless.
Don't be tame, sheeple,
don't be tame.
You're the one!
Go out while you can
and have some fun!

etheridge knight

i

Why come this far
through the bars
of your cell
only to write a poem,
they would needle him.

ii (his voice)

Gathering up my wits
against my self-destructive tendencies
won't insure I won't lose them again
but I'll be damned if I give up trying
So here are some words to shore up
against, as been said, the ruins
in rhythm I can stomach, in diction
plain and simple, in tone fierce
and mournful and full of love
for this hellish warring world
words I won't waste a syllable of.

shuntaro tanikawa

After we came back
from interviewing him
at his house in Tokyo
my wife said to me:

His body is so full
of power and energy.

He doesn't waste
a moment
and capitalizes on
every opportunity.

He's like a monk
trained at a higher level
or plane of existence
than the rest of us.

And I thought of Bruce Lee
famously saying:
Be water, my friends. –

And remembered
Miles Davis saying
Be wrong, strong. –

Then interjected the line
from Japan's best-known living poet—
I'm a short, bald-headed old man.

Only later did I read:
I know who I am,
so I also know who you are.
Even if I don't know your name

linda pastan

—after *Queen of a Rainy Country*

Before I knew what my life would bring—
lightning at thirty when reading Dante's
sky; a son at thirty-one in cold December;
a resettlement at thirty-two in my wife's
native land, now going on thirty years—
I knew I wanted to sing, regardless of
the sound of my voice. Let the stories
tell themselves, I thought, while music
hold the single note lost to a melody
I would call the world's. And before
I knew what my death would require—
dust from the famished feast of the past;
a future visible by a vanishing trail;
the present letting go its only wish—
I knew I would speak its language
of desire, tasking me irrevocably higher.

sylvia plath

Sylvia, Sylvia, the (imagined) Jew in you cracked,
taking the bait of history no myth could
withstand. *Zeig Heil!* was what you got
an earful of, sad to say, but you ran with
it all the way to your death that keeps
giving, years later, to readers of poet-trees
such as me, who climb carefully one
branch at a time to see what you saw:
see-saw for the little ones? hee-haw
for the subtle ones? re-caw for the
misfit ones that we are, witches et al?
Spellbound you were, and made us all
become, footloose and fancy freed.
The dead you walked with broke
you bad, I'd say, and woke you a tad
further on the path to Plath, zero-
houred in the gas-lit dawn's early light.

mark strand

i

The man the moon made up
hammered a life in the sun.
He drew down the light
in rays that shone on the page
like stars. He drank the nectar
of night like milk, and swept
away his dreams into the bin
of dawn, where he rose illusion-
free and smiling. The world was
real enough without his shadow
passing over it, yet what that
was eluded him unless, yes,
the words he heard could color
in the contours of his melancholy
one dark laugh-line at a time, now
fashioned into forms he could bear.

ii (his voice)

I slid into the maneuvers of wanting
what I never thought I could sing
and found the underneath sound of it
pulling me forward. There came what
I understood was the subject at hand
word by word, and deeper than the end.
I slowed the journey down for where
it led me, control the least of it, care

the most of it, for the middle way
which allowed me to have my say.

iii

It's a tough titty but
we all gotta suck on it,
was a favorite saying
of the late poet Mark Strand.

iv on his passing

Mr. Strand had stars aplenty in
his orbit. He advanced a comic vision
hidden beneath a veneer of pessimism,
and from a young age harbored ambition
to become a painter. A stalwart
defender of poetry, he sought out
new palettes of written genres
late in his career. Strand, a Canadian,
lived his adult life in the U.S.
In its culture of victim-ing, he took
on all comers with deadpan wit.
His poetic opus, *The Monument*,
is just that. His brilliant work will outlive him.

mary oliver

i.m. 1935-2019

i

She invented a way of seeing
the mind at work in nature,
her perceptions growing in faith
and devotion—forms of attention
by her own lights—and with her
poetic reflections we see more clearly
into the mystery of change, deeper
in nature, for her, than in the historical
Resurrection. She bears careful
witness and exhumes herself out
from under the dark despair that
haunts the outer precincts of her
poetry, if not her mind, and keeps
us, her readers, close by her on her
journey, a profoundly shared love
of the natural world being her unwavering
compass, and ours too. Within her
language is created a world redeemed
by forms of attention available to us all.
Opening new territory by a cartography
of spirit, she won't chase things down
the rabbit hole of imagination, but
delivers things whole by becoming
part of all she sees.

ii — after *Upstream* (her voice)

We honor the dead in our heads
but in our hearts, we love them
more than words can say. This
is what the dead have taught me,
and will you, too, if you let them.
We cancel no debt lengthwise
or widthwise, only in their
circumference of our souls do we
come into true contact with them,
and that is all the treatment our
souls require to stay alive. We
yield to its measure of fire earth
air and water, and other elements
besides. The dead rehearse for us
the spiritual journey on which we
embark, from the palpable to the
ephemeral and beyond. It is no
exaggeration to say that they give
us our life its inner harmonies,
such music as we hear in the
magnificent solitude any work
of great art conspires to construct,
I dare say on false pretenses too,
since the truth is always erotic,
always an involvement or immersion
in what takes us further out of ourselves
and closer to the God within us. Such
is the artist's paradox, on the back
of which we willingly, thrillingly
ride. I swoon in the arms of the world
they died for. And humbly live for it, too.

iii she addresses her Muse

Through your eyes and ears, Poet,
I dance on the shore of timelessness.
Through your voice I travel
the seas of eternity and death
is but a diversion at dawn.
Through your words I come
to my senses pure as fine-spun gold.
Such tales as you tell sound
the depths I cherish growing old.
Denizen of the deep, yours is
the redeeming call, barring none.
I've sought its tenor as guide to
the ineffable, which I've learned
to be life's only outlasting truth.

iv The Owl (her voice)

The owl's terror-bringing beak
and claws have a Moses-like
thunder as the lawgiver of
death in life, that I shudder
at the sight, majestic and
proud, of their hunt, which
I know to be non-stop and
dune-heavy above the ponds
where I amble, eyes peeled
for the feathered archangel.

v The Gull (her voice)

There are birds in one's life
that go on flying forever. One such

gull touched my heart, and I have
seen a portion of sky like no other.
He rang the bell inside me that
to this day resonates with soft
affection and tender mercy, and but
for the hardness of the fact of his death
that I have nailed down for you
in words, I would have still his
companionship to this day, loyal
nursemaid that am I, cum birdwatcher.
How often I felt him watching us
and lighting upon our lives with
a mischievous and knowing eye.

vi Her crucible

The pleasures of this poet are perhaps too
tempting, too full of heavenly blossoms
to stay long in her orbit—with the natural
world her crucible—yet who can
resist the pure flux of yes no she
mastered for herself, for her life,
for us, her readers, she holding nothing
back not even the rapture of
death she waded in, unafraid,
solitary self stripped of recognitions
save those found in undying change,
one she made sing for the sea-changes
she bathed in, O pool of Apollonian poetry
fed by Dionysian streams she followed
to their source in her gifted, gifting heart.

*

She had another sixteen years to live
when at sixty-seven she wrote of
the meadowlark with such lavish attention
that under its whistle-call she opened
like a bud, finding its voice in gratitude.

*

Revving up, it seems (in hindsight), for her big
send-off, she came out of hiding towards the end,
giving interviews and readings, doing recordings,
publishing a steady stream of new books,
until when her time came, she left a felt void
perhaps calculated to be filled by her words,
her great gift to us, a voice of lived beauties—
days and days and days of them.

charles wright

— after "Body and Soul"

Which is it—body?
or soul? —he doesn't say,
but in not saying it,
    we know
how the shadows part
   for the word writ
large, or small, in a script
   that counts for
the world, were we
   not erased in the writing
of it, we who leave selves
we were for selves we become,
  languaging our bodies
into being, or trying to,
the sky the stars shine in
   the pages we turn
for the stories we read
   in our sleep.

lucille clifton

The times riven with tears were hers
to lament to witness to record the same
as now how different are they the times
we live in she knew this and wrote for heirs.

*

Astringent, sly and slow
to make herself known
to the reader, whom
she disinvites
on the hook
of her lines, reeling
you in nice
and easy into
the net of
hope.

june jordan

— after 'For the Sake of People's Poetry'

(her voice)

I love Whitman's poetry beyond
the stretch of his New World imagination,
for there isn't any poet of the past
who conjoins with the future as
beautifully or as effortlessly as
he does. He waits for his reader,
wherever she or he is, as if for a friend,
and placates no inward frothing of
freedom, as his own inward seas
cannot be quelled, try as the Old World
mindset does to quell it. He swells
and impregnates the English language, too,
whose offspring can still be heard and will
never be quieted. He unleashes
the moon and sun and stars within
each of us, and opens vistas that keep
on opening into the New, wherever
it might lead. He assuages no guilt,
inculcates no shame in his stretching
forth, always both humble and proud.
Dante's spark might have leapt the gap
but Whitman's fire rages across time's
wilderness to clear a free space where men
and women can live unbowed, equal partners.

(You won't rue having
read June Jordan.)

c.k. williams

i (his voice)

The lilt of the back-ended phrase advances
the line out over the edge of the visible
and then, pulling up, lingers there in a dance
with whatever I can make real to myself,
which is no easy feat, I find, no matter
the detail hit upon, no matter the rhythm
sounded from unseen depths. I resort,
then, to the efficacy of my fears to clear
a path forward into the abyss, a home
this time around where space contracts
and the horizon recedes… Now I am gone
over ever deeper, further than I can imagine,
where all ethical considerations vanish
into the sum of the next decision's parts
I waste no time in forsaking, rightly or
wrongly letting appearances have
the final word, one I knew all along.

ii

He was tall,
dressed all
in black.
He commanded
the stage,
and from where

I sat I thought,
I can do that.

Forty years later
I read his poems
one by one
and think,
what gall
I had.

iii (his voice)

What pill ever swallowed
alleviates the pain we bear.
How does the power of desire
ever release you from its
clutches to return you to
a state of innocence without
a permanent stain on the heart
of, call it circumstance,
or call it your integrity?
I am transformed, is what you
say when the signal's been
given, when the way
has been cleared and you
find yourself, undeservedly, in
a state of grace which in itself
in a heartbeat reverts to
being a state of spiritual entropy
the moment you believe what you say,
your words as if out of a dream
you'll awaken from into a language
of others you imagine are real,

or have their roots in reality,
from which grows a self
you have no way of knowing
isn't already passing beyond
this mind you've written
long after the change took place
that made you look at your life
and the others in it
from a distance, remembered,
infused with bystander's guilt,
standing in the field of these interchangings.

iv (his voice)

You could not have been in your right mind
going left, but having ended up here where
you have left behind all doubts and misgivings,
now knowing somehow, you were right all along.

The news from books has brought me untold satisfaction.
Not the result of any psychic power on my part, but
their dreams being replayed over and over in my head
to be layered with my consciousness to create
always something mysterious and new.

Decades ago, extreme views predominated, but now
they wend in and out of the national conversation
that we have no way of knowing will last.

The wizard of darkness is not powerful, though
intoning the spells brings him closer to the light
to reveal a man with perhaps a hollow heart
burning with lust, aching for bliss, invoking

the mysteries. Whether I am that man or not
depends on an ethical imagination others
have wearied of my having, insisting as it does
on crossing boundaries at the edges of waking
and sleep, a place where the stakes are high.
For the burden of reality I carry with me
as I make my way alone, always alone,
is for and towards others on my quest for,
what else, love, singing for no other reason
than for love.

v (his voice)

I put down the book on war
and dove into the one for
the morally impugned of us
by the evils of the world, lust-
driven and blood-soaked, again
the poet's nomenclature but in
the employ of hidden desires gun-
ning for the way things are, a target
for all his anger, his fury, his bitter
rage which in time grows wiser
but no less embittered, the past a place
he revisits, mining memories for their
pathos and wit lest he forget how
the human in him, his humanity, got
the way it did, gone to the dogs, the dogs
of war who guard the gates not
of hell, nor of hate, nor of the hardening
heart but, it seems, of the drama of being.

vi

…Listen, I have important things
to do, so will you please leave?...

Steamrolled out of his life
were the children
he sought out in old age,
his poetry begetting the experience
of forgetting innocence enough to
pretend it never existed to begin with,
a strategy that seemed to work
except for the fact that he needed
the innocence for his moral compass
—without which he was lost—
the innocence that charged beauty
with power, forming its lifeblood.

eleanor wilner

Storms… Storms…

Who cares?

…History does. For all time…
For 'he' it was who told
the stories she wanted
to hear, or thought she did,
until the lid was lifted from
the world she had known
and would give anything to keep.
He told stories she had grown
by and from and laid down in,
and so help her god she would
repeat them now as if her life
depended on it, which it did, she
being not only tourist in hell
but teller all along,
her voice an echo of his,
a wind in the trees.

alicia ostriker

—after *The Volcano and After*

The trail of tears isn't long
before it belongs to the story she tells
in fits and starts, the one her heart
can't find the words to, that wells
up in the season of her winter song.

The bleeding heart bleeds on the page
her years gone by, done in by
a generation marching to the savage
drumbeat of the self that will not die.
The bleeding heart bleeds on the page
her tears fallen; her dreams stolen
from the perilous deeps of her age
that hell paves in a vanished heaven.

She cringes at the slow approaching of death
but sings each note with breath
distilled through her love of language
containing one not-so-secret message:
that despite it all, the wars
and whores and unopened doors,
the weight lifted   and carried her
closer to the Light   of her Higher
Being.   And that was enough.

stephen dunn

i

The poet houses mystery in a roomful
of words, stanza by stanza revealing
what isn't there for the taking, locked
away it is behind an attitude, a formal
feeling being expressed despite itself,
for the benefit of the show he'll yet make
much of, quietly hidden within himself
as only the holy is, applause lines
notwithstanding, that make stars appear.
This the magic of the poem, darkly seen
and heard, felt as a lamp turning on,
drinks being poured, everyone settling in.

ii

His poems sit up straight now,
calling to me like an old friend
I haven't talked to for ages, and we
get down to the business of sussing each
other out, trying once again to believe
the world doesn't have it in for us,
perhaps even wishes us well. They
sit up, as certain poems will do, when
leaning forward to whisper ever so gently
in your ear, their words now finally spoken,
shaped to perfection, given the imperfect
arc that wheels around abruptly near their end,

the one planned for all along, the one
the poet gives his eye-teeth for, the one
his savvy art invites before he's done.

iii —after *Degrees of Fidelity*

(his voice)

While I was alive, I didn't hanker after
posterity and its supposed blandishments.
I stayed within my limits, satisfied that
I had attained my goals, such as they were,
as a writer of poems I could be proud of,
poems that never strayed outside
the ken of the human, would not alter
the facts to fit an idealized truth, and
didn't tempt fate beyond the occasional
flight of imagination which excess allows
you when the inner censor stops censoring.
Now, in my afterlife, I can look back
and feel the weight of my accomplishments
with no small pride, yet with humility, too,
since my failures are what my life fits into
snugly, like a foot inside a sock or a shoe,
and here, may I never outwear my welcome.

william heyen

— after *The Candle*

i

He won't betray what history
compels him to say, no matter
what the cost (to others or himself),
no matter how brutal the story. History
communes with the dead,
he says, by means of spirit
that, incarnating, turns into smoke
smoldering out of chimneystacks
or into bodies, vaporized, that leave
shadows in their places, whole cities
of them, swarming to be heard.

ii (his voice)

History has a way of being
History has a way of killing
History has a way of bordering
on the profane and sacred
to make corpses of us all
and I am here to tell it so
to tell it thus to tell it by
self-indictment and criminal
blood staining my pages
which I make for the sake
of a beauty that aches

with and for stories I will tell
lest I rot in hell wordless
as the victims I invoke

iii (his voice)

This may be my first,
I mean my best
in praise of the worst
of humanity. Of history,
yes, a test.

Read it
and weep, our shared 20th century fates
that I've dared to look deep inside of. The fake
moralists will cringe at what they see, I
guarantee. And the truth within my sights
I aim for— no gun-lover, I— will never be the same.

iv — after *Yawp: Heyen's Whitman*

(his voice)

Heyen here, with a story to tell
of our beloved Walt, no saint it turns
out but malevolence itself personified,
his poem no exception, violating us
in the guise of elevating us, and we
his victims reading 'our' song of myself
he sang to belong tooth and nail
to posterity he was courting all along,
the textual body he bellowed forth
was, it seems, not above exploiting

desire of every stripe to win the judgment
of history in his favor, at the reader's
expense, the one propelling him there.
(Or will this murky connection to the Bard
put us in mind of a deeper unity
we can find within us, shared as no
golden hoard can be, here declared
by no word of mine, jointly heard.)

v — after *Yawp: Heyen's Whitman*

(his voice)

No politics the poet speaks can compare
with the vision of nature inherent in his words
which we, in our contemporaneity, imbibe
through our pores into the deepest part of
our longing to believe and praise, past the
horrors outlived, the griefs implacable as
the dust wreathing every light peace inspires,
as we, sleepers all, awaken now to the union
that will never not be and is re-aligned
in the space of a poem written in the heart,
one whose chambers flowing with blood
pump its meanings from the particulars of Walt's art
that lives on in the wholeness and fullness of time
called, were it not too late nor too little, the soul,
in derisive and divine laughter summoned here
through temporal shadow, breath of night.

joseph brodsky

With certain poets, like Joseph Brodsky, to be in their presence was to be energized.

The bluff and the growl, those were Joseph's staples.

Any area to which he contributed he wanted to own.

In a dream… a panoramic vision comes to me of all the various images of Brodsky—sad, weeping, reciting passionately, laughing—just as I remembered and admired him during the time I studied under him. A voice says: "There's nothing to steal in life." A student calls him up later and asks him: "Who's the ghost with the most?" And Joseph replies: "That's the question this test will answer. Let the games begin."

ii (his voice)

The crow caws its applause
as the clouds sway and rise
above the darkness, seemingly,
of the day, toxic to the degree
that it claims a new subliminal
territory in your consciousness,
which is anything but communal.
So keep your eyes and ears open
to the breezes and thermals passing
by your way, weather patterns
the sun and the moon reminiscing
make upon the sky crossing

on their rounds, maddening and diurnal.
Let the cerebral cortex soundly
return you to the hard thought
time insists your being taught,
weighted in space beautifully
where the grass seems untrampled
and the city, perhaps, is unpeopled.
Let the more loving one be you
if only for the ample, indifferent view
and to hear when being spoken to,
if also to bear being unheard,
what is the promised word
between me and you.

iii meeting Joseph Brodsky, again

I thought you had died,
I told him in my dream,
and he looked surprised
(I watched his eyebrows rise).
How busy he looked,
talking as night fell— now
to the old man from
Eastern Europe, now
on the phone to the elderly
female translator who
had questions to ask, now
sitting at the café table
with the young writer holding
in his hands a book
whose title I could see
(but not now), the look
on his face reflecting

the seriousness on Joseph's, the delight
to discuss this or that during this
Cafe Reggio *tete-a-tete.*
The young writer had one
eye bulging wider
than the other (what could
that have meant, I wondered)
as all around us the night
grew ever darker, ever darker.

iv At a time of war (to J.B.)

Outside the window the neighbor's rooftop
dove-bedecked antennae hums
in the ear as I recall the nocturnal
visit by you, offering to me a poem,
'At a Time of War' that upon waking
I search for. But
the journey is far, Joseph, and away

the wave-soaked, sea-borne spirit
you brought to life, where strife reins
in thoughts of craft's continuing
past a noonday chill and no angels
gather to sing of or lament
the battles to come. I ought
to be grateful the road has led

here. War-cries abound, yet I won't
be around when somebody or
other wins, hands down. Victory
is not a space I dwell in. Defeat,
like loss, I'm at home in. Let

words furnish the emptiness.
Or not. Either way, I'll welcome

you there in the longing's quiet.
The poet doesn't need a mountain
to stand on, nor ceremony. The hill
I'm at the foot of is your name
reaching the sun, shadowless
as no memory is, no matter how fond.
Clinical valor in a time of war
is the caveat of art. Yours—art
and valor—keep breaking
the mind from its cave free.

v. The Brodsky memoirist

— after Ellendea Proffer Teasley's *Brodsky Among Us*

(her voice)

Poets like you and me have nothing
on poets of genius like Joseph Brodsky,
whose flight into exile propelled him far
into the stratospheres of fame and
recognition. Yet it must be said he
was far, too, from being an exemplary man,
rather ordinary in his desires and
flaws, which here I won't make much
of except to say he was one who could
be quickly forgiven his transgressions.
Friendship with him had to be worked at,
it's true, but always reaped rewards.
With him in the picture it was a bigger
world. With him in one's heart, pure heat.

vi Exile

A Dante, a salt-taster of another's bread,
a treader of another's stairs, he made
his way to the stars step by step, ahead
of the curve of time arcing through space,
sighing intermittently, lonely to the end:
What did you do before you died, is
the matter, he'd said, irrevocably at hand,
for which one always pays a price.

vii (his voice)

The zeros you place before and after your name
places eternity and infinity squarely without blame.
You face both on a dare that lasts a lifetime
of refusing, not denying, the easy rhyme
to come back to whatever you'd call home.
Either way, the future gives you its spellings
in a dictation you have no choice but to write
down by heart, heard as an uninterrupted sound that rings
true whether in the end darkness outshines the light.

viii

A poet gone too soon, celebrated in
his lifetime Brodsky was, though.

To please a shadow
must be easier to do than
to embrace a spirit.

robert haas

— after "Meditation on Lagunitas"

The desire he deems valuable
envelops the soul in delight
so all-encompassing that
it falls in love with pain
in the hereafter, a gift
nobody can ever take
away from you. He says
the way he remembers her
transforms the voice in its
telling, into a story one'll tell
time and time again which no
listener can tire of, no reader
can mistake—for the climax
undoes language at the seams
where sound dissolves into meditative sense
and you become the words spoken
afterwards, which grief will embody,
her name notwithstanding, in
those moments passing for eternity,
in praise of which you'll sing,
letting each wistful note take you
tenderly through the lost years
back to her, back to her, back to her.

hiroaki sato

(his voice)

The debt we owe you—that is you,
the reader—the writer struggles to repay.
What residue of that interaction lingers
in the mind, nay, even heart, helps
keep us human, despite the pain.
Or maybe because of it. No wisdom
I claim, just a front-row seat to
the name-game we moderns play,
leaving us in constant mourning, I say.
The ancients knew better, and rued
the day the word was 'made flesh'.
Fresher pastures, they knew, lie ahead
of the backward-glancing eye
that 360 degrees sees the sphere of our
locomotion the tear-stained face,
now wet, now dry, keeps turning to,
a rhythmic beat drumming messages
night and day that orient us, east
or west, toward our meaning…

For the mind's coping mechanism cannot
always maintain its desired equilibrium.
That is why we need metaphor—
that swerve away from the unconscious
and toward the reality-making function
we rely on, past the violence of dream images.
Yet it seems to me those dreams—

the very Siren songs Ulysses 3000 years ago
had to fortify himself against—are the origins
of all creative endeavor, giving rise
to our human need to tell stories.

sharon olds

i

We're starved for effort
to come our way, to say
things we need to hear.
We make do with less
for lack not of trying
but of listening.

*

She dialed in to ordinary mind
to find what's extraordinary
about it—the ways we love and
deceive one another, the ways
we hold on and let go and move on.
She tells women's tales in particular,
dismissing critics of her blood-soaked,
female-embodied work, saying her
romance with the body is key,
the model of escape and return
the primal directives.
Look where matters have gone
in her poems, how opened the heart is,
that the naughty and satanic receive
a hearing. This release offered is
the only way we can see
our lives unblighted.

ii (her voice)

I have not been well
enough to climb out of hell
when I had half a chance,
when I embarked on a dance
with the devil, gleeful
in his fiery circumstance,
having baited me with smoke
and mirrors, until stuck
on him, on this angelic lover
of mine, begging him lower,
lower, to waltz him dark
through the gate of trance.

iii

To what she owned she would give
her allegiance, total and absolute, as she
would claim her suffering, her pleasure,
her bitterness, her game. She would not lose
what she owned, not herself, unless to
another in her soul's belonging, total and
absolute, even or especially if they brought
a taste of her own poison, now satisfied
she could bear it all again.

iv

In the miasma of the embodied she lingers
long, to sing the mammalian rites, entrances
into the cult of the female mysteries and trials
that are to be humanly borne, to satisfy

the desire to be reborn through the canal
of words, of womb-carried vessels of spirit
ecstatically spoken, hungrily heard, a curtain
lifted on what tears the flesh into original,
pain-opened pity for the unconditional in us,
call it love, that calls us down into incarnated
truth, undeniable, that offers no
shelter from where it will take us, alone,
when we exit, God-like, into the mind
newly equipped for the unknown
to which she surrenders, swooning,
every word her touchstone.

v

Hell hath no fury than a poet
writing perfectly calibrated
poems cut on confession's teeth,
cerebral snarl and growl disguised
as rhythm and metaphor,
as Cerberus jealously guarding
the gates, keeping the dead in
line, and spiritually end-stopped,
until her Hercules in a labor
of love, twists the three-headed
one into a mystery we didn't see
coming, but was there all along,
heroine of her life and ours.

vi ars poetica

(her voice)

You click the link and off you go,
not knowing where, on a dare
to the next and the next and so on
connecting one thing to another,
processing and retrieving, testing
until a pattern emerges, one you
can surmise was there all along,
were you able to see. And seeing
it now emboldens you to cross
over to the other side of the decision
you've made to follow where
it leads you, to meanings fallow
as if in fields of barely contained
expertise, digging deep into error
and postulation, terror even,
far from incidental, at its core
what you've aimed for, to borrow
not a phrase but real power, yours now,
one that line after line unravels
like the thread out of a labyrinth
of your own making, staking
your very life on getting out
in time, before the beast in you
catches on, and the beauty dies.

doug anderson

— after *The Moon Reflected Fire*

(his voice)

I've sun-soaked verses to redeem the shitstorms
I've survived, no bloodlust but has boiled over in
the heat of battles that belittled men as much as
glorified them, both of which I've seen plenty.

Now the pitfalls are ones a poet escapes, with lingo
all his own. He rocks the tightened wire that
he walks on, to the tune of war, or brutal love,
or both at once, cruel beyond measure of song.

sam hamill

i

He stuns.
They shun…
…Another day
under a lonely
sun.
Such a long
way to go.
Poetry is
no money tree.

ii

'Sam', hammered and tempered
in the flame, the mysteries mind
comprehends momentarily remixed
as reminiscence of what he'd find,
mellowed with the moonlight
shining down on him, his mate
preceding his footsteps to the grave,
him calling out to her every step of the way.

louise gluck

(her voice)

Male mastery of
female mystery is
commensurate with neither
thought nor feeling—
such is the *agon* of style,
all hell of the wrong gods
broken loose in the mind,
the genres of who we are
trying so hard to be. Not some star
in the firmament we'll never reach,
were we ever to mount that high,
but its melodic equivalent where
stripped of time and place, the view
of music is a windfall of the eternal
longing for what one can't have.
Give me grace notes, trills, glissandos (and all that jazz)
that resonate in a place all their own, however,
and I'll have belonging's name uttered,
if not unfettered,
by these lips for now.

*

I brought up the edge to my feet
by looking into, not away, from
others, satisfying the need
to materialize concretely by

rehearsing immortality, that home
the I constructs, over and over,
returned to after death the self
stages by degrees, absent the seed
the ground welcomes, being
by any other name. This the fame
won from the void, were we
hungry for it in the body. Let
spirit, instead, haunt me
for otherness not to forget
its origin, its genius as world
without an end, without a word
in me, painstakingly, to say it so.

*

What have I come to but this
that were I able to describe thus
without succumbing to doubt, would
free me of faith's particulars, world
emptied of its burning chill
that marks the journey, say what we will,
for it's what we do that sees us through
the darkness entered, past the rose's view.

*

Happy to get through the night,
you will yourself awake
to reason another day.
It travels with you in sight
of all the things that make
you wish you had a different way,

yet you hold to the line
that gives you the only sign
you need, once again, to realign,
and so you have your say
despite not having your cake
and eating it too—albeit lived through—
the taste of which strikes you
as being evidence of the snake
in your garden, the manifesting mistake
that is the only tale worth telling
that others, you hope, find worth hearing.

Part Four

alfred corn

i (his voice)

Forty-some years of
photos, and years of
fighting them.
It's fixed me up
with a face I wear,
but do I care
what others think?
I do. A face to
share on Facebook, don't you know,
where we go to read the
expressions on other people's
faces and in the books of
their inscrutable lives.

ii (his voice)

Time to consider consciousness.

But don't space out on us.

Here we go: Whose body is
on my mind right now as I speak
and whose mind is embodying
these words as I peek?
Paying mind is what my body
does, for free. We enjoy the company.
If I'm paying no mind to your body,

you'd be hard-pressed to be
re-embodied after the fact. Fact is,
without a body, mind is fucked.
Without a mind, body does it
all for naught. Not much to go
on, I'll say. Mind seconds body's
motion and keeps energies in play.

That's consciousness, raised by
the body of mine.

aram saroyan

What does the cricket sing?
Being, being being

james tate

Facing the absurdity of his ending,
he gave the last rites to himself,
and pronounced himself afraid.
Who wouldn't be? He gave
the last rites to himself again,
and declared himself brave,
who wouldn't not try to be.

annie dillard

(her voice)

If you're feeling lonely, at least make some noise.
Breakfast in a shoebox won't do. Lay your spread
on a table wide as the world and eat. There's your hunger
not to be satisfied, there's your thirst not to be slaked
except in the doing, now your loneliness assuaged.

Unscrew the doors from their jambs! said Whitman
while scribbling away in his room. If however the poetry
won't fit in your time, it will come after, or at least that's
the chance you must take. If the time fits you, so much
the better, but that is rare. Make room for time and history
in the auto-corrective business you're in, your salient
mistakes lighting the path ahead. Spirit of the journalist Jew
where any misstep may be unwise, or even fatal, but risking it all
is nevertheless what you do. (He's not fascinated with gigs
unless danger rises to meet him on his way, one slip and it's
over.)

When eating the watermelon you spit the seeds out,
holding the rind in your hands. Summer never tasted any better.

kay ryan

i

Slow reform can teach us
quickly what it costs
not to change when
opportunity comes knocking
at your door, door to
the future making history
for us all
who are thirsty
for awakenings,
dying to move,
to make headway
true to life,
as this team talk
above and below,
of new airwaves.

ii

Opening a path to
where she won't go
is quite a show—
it's what she will do
given half a dance,
partnering with ur-circumstance
to the degree it allows,
while implacable follows
unpredictable, to close

what expectations defy,
effortlessly, and on the fly.

iii

Something precisely said
invites not its own extinction
but the extinction of its reason for being:
The liberated mind ripped
into the unsaid.

yusef komunyakaa

—on a poem of his

(his voice)

In the trammeled byways
of the outsider blues, I'm at home

In the weed-filled backyards
of tenement buildings, I'm at home

At the furthest edge of
the note-filled nights
whose letters go unanswered,
I'm at home

In the unheralded dawn
where the suicides line up
and outwait eternity to be reborn,
I'm at home

I'm at home
till the chickens leave
their roosts in the shadow
of the sun. And then I'm gone.

gregory orr

i —after *The Last Love Poem I Will Ever Write*

Nothing could move him
into the depths
like emotion
where he swam
to where the tide rips
a lesser man
to pieces, or did
as he regathered himself
by lines he wrote
to try and stay afloat—
a chance to build
his own ship
now his best hope,
a craftsman skilled
beyond words,
he obeying the winds
in the end, that led
him to shores he could
never have seen
or imagined before, island
of his dark, sinister world,
his beloved, broken world
lived in long
and deep, under
a wave all along
he'd call song.

ii —after *River Inside the River*

(his voice)

Out of the morass
the mysteries,
out of the mysteries
more of us
to story, no end
but fits a beginning
lost to time,
found in rhyme,
pleasure indemnified
that we won't hide
away, pain notwithstanding,
a song to sing
for the Friend,
she or he on whom
we depend.

*

I watch where it goes,
this river of words,
—river of grief, river of praise—
following where it flows
into newer worlds
I won't be going to,
except when I'm through.

*

The city I'll have made
my second home
in, will welcome me
after I'm gone. That's good
enough for me,
for now.
For those who come
after will see
my place, if not my face,
through the doorway
these words open.
Let the dead have their say,
I will tell them
as they enter,
even as I write this,
even as you read this.

ellen bass

i — after *Like a Beggar*

(her voice)

The earth's got reasons of its own—
call them seasons—that do us in eventually,
the cankered bodies we drag around
not the least of it, boding well or ill,
of things to come.
We anticipate the daily scourge of time
breaking down our defenses, but O what
lines we pumped into the world from
the heart we hide ourselves in, what
poems we sent out into the cosmic fray
whose dust we are! How our repose
in the face of it could overtake all but
the speediest fate bringing down Babel,
were it here toppled to eye-level,
where we can see into the mystery
and, falling to our knees, feel a bitter-
sweet triumph at last setting us free
to sing, sing, sing of sexuality,
the tongue and parted lips and teeth
wildly, tenderly praising the territory
once forbidden, now opened, the Temple
visited every evening to keep the candles
lit, I the shamash light, she who kindles
the other lights, raised up high, set apart,
servant of our earthly, beautiful pain.

ii —after *Indigo*

It's distinctive, her beauty, American
in its soulfulness that honors the thatness
of the body, the wonders of its wantings,
the starry shade of its mysteries she
sings, with mouth open to all the losses
she's borne, that she carries within her
as the gifts they are, turning her inside
out when the time comes, when words
filter through the love she feels for
what is hers and hers alone, flesh
and blood bewildering in its detail,
storied as only children can be, offspring
of her imagination grown entirely
familiar, the world married
marking its truths deep in her art,
grief-powered and joy-veined,
the palpable, the mournful, the willful, the proud
bearing of surrender (but not yet), exchanging
the ticket on the bet she made, the gamble
that pays off in increments, daily winnings
she's still collecting, the dead she bows down to
lifting her up into the amniotic sunlight
where all she is, and isn't, is seen
for who she is, the kiss of life
Germany had tried to burn in the camps,
seeing to it it is preserved in the push
of imagination, unblocked
by memory she rides to the death,
the one awaiting her like a star.

yoko danno

(her voice)

The dream dangles before me its wispy meanings
while thunder rolls beneath the words, and lightning
strikes the mind enmeshed in the storyline we would
give it, were we on the path to an ending, which
we're not, but starting at the beginning leads us
to new places I wish my words could convey,
that borderland I visit every now and then, keen
on seeing what we'll see in the darkness before dawn.

takako arai

It augers well the sound the well makes
when she calls down into it, voice
reverberating across its walls deep
in shadow, reverberating across the surface
of the water inside, a clear source
of nourishment for whomever comes
after, they who would haul up from
its depths the water to drink, to slake
the thirst that has led them there, the well
she keeps watch over, protective, maternal,
sharp-eyed and honest, who turns
her language into the shape of the well
out of which lines come forth, channeling
what's hidden there, passages
cool, clear, and inexhaustible.

yuri kageyama

(her voice)

I was not someone, they'll say
of me, who wandered around
and got lost in the crowd. I've had
to say my say the way I've said it
for people to sit up and take notice.
Or I'm just another Asian ho
in their eyes. No regrets
I always say, let your enemies
say what they will.

c.d. wright

—after a poem of hers

(her voice)

Living was my go-to theme
when dying made the decisions.
I would go to bat for living
but got saddled with dying
as my vehicle of choice.
Living had me going in circles
when dying was a line I crossed.
It was living that saved my ass
how many times, from simply
dying, light or no light.
Living around here affords
the simplest pleasures,
and witnessing the dying
is one of them,
in an unmorbid way.
No seed under the breath
taunting the tongue, I
cut my teeth on living.
The hours spent growing
sentences in the garden
of my body, under
the sunlight of soul,
was my loving
living as I do.

david rigsbee

— after *Not Alone in My Dancing*

i

What he brings to bear
is the world's perishability
on the poet's penchant for
renewal in spite of, or because
of it—always pitched as a
contest less of wills, and more
of imagination and surrender
to the exigencies of writing itself,
words on a page carrying on
the work of instigating change
one mind at a time.

ii The duelist (his voice)

What do we want if not the most
from our time on earth—that host
we ride inseparably from, as a guest
the other side of forever who'll insist
on being taken there in a test
of endurance, of who will best
whom for eternity's sake, to dust
off lasting fame by being, yes, first
to draw the other into withdrawing,
for time's sake, into this mortal singing,
though History, the debt-collector, resist
all but business as usual's come due list.

iii The poet-critic (his voice)

I aver to the Tradition and confer
with its practitioners and refer to
its precursors (for whom it answered
a higher calling), but will confer
the moniker 'poet' sparingly
on those who've earned it the
hard way—in the trenches where
the *agon* has been fought for
millennia, centuries of experience
that, it's true, I display or, if you
prefer, show off— mojo by any
other name by which poetry is
made, make no mistake. I'll
go to any lengths to outwit and
outwrite an opponent, on or off
the page, for writing is what I do
best, and criticism too, whose
mastery I command. Respectability,
whether yearned for or earned, is
the bottom-line for poet-tasters
and geniuses alike. My view
of things will change the day
Poetry dies, which they've been
predicting forever. Until then, I'll write
it and talk about it for as long as we
both shall live, so help me Prometheus.

john skoyles

i (his voice)

We remember the moments of our lives
best in images brought to bear by the poet
in poems made for the ages, if they last
that long. But emerging through the fog
of forgetfulness are certain moments captured
just so, by which our destinies play out,
contingencies manifest themselves, and
judgments are passed, rendering the past
with brushstrokes intended to conflate
the cosmic with the meaningless, the fray
more navigable, if provisionally,
between syntax and its artifacts, faith
and desire, soul and body. To see what
exactly? A doting husband, a lone poet
spending his life on words that never get
any closer to the language of the heart
he has learned, in so many words, to forget
to cancel in the darkening violence of our age.

ii (his voice)

It was desire I courted
from the past I inherited,
desire to fornicate being
the least of it; rather,
desire for more life,
that blessing from the

Angel wrestled in the night
day after day, always pulling
me toward the other side
of memory, were I free
of its hold, were I aware
of its power to change
the view from the inside, where
I've taken up residence,
cognizant of the time remaining
to me, in a world
of desires I never wanted
satisfied to begin with,
only to feel each one
fully rounded in the end
by my squaring off
at the root of it all,
on which my heart
was set.

eileen myles

(her voice)

Mines thinly
disguised as lines:
Watch your step.
Pride needs
to be prodded in
new directions, free style…
Sticking to the facts for
the butterfly effect.

*

Straightforward it isn't, this 'poetry' stuff,
full of twists and burns, teeterings on
the brink, abysmal falls rough
on the sense of self, come and gone
through fires galore, walls too,
inward routes that keep one true
to the times we live in, whose spaces
open onto the neglected places
underneath the 'appearances'…But no more
are we to knock on this door
(she said, with a roar).

*

Build unity
through art?

There's nothing
unifying about art.
Save as unity
of thought and emotion.

*

(History as a debt to break free of
requires a good debt counselor.
The poet is your man.)

jorie graham

i (her voice)

You tell too much and the storyline
collapses, you tell too little
and the storyline won't take hold.
Safer to say what goes
away than what stays, if
anything, for that is the lie
of permanence you don't want
to be called out on, since
passing away is what
sooner or later everything does, even
spells made up of blossoming words
that know where they're
going before they get there,
distanced from what is loved,
a stand taken in what passes
with desire given in spades.

ii (her voice)

Around our opaque
puzzleuniversities,

drop the gloves.

adele ne jame

i (her voice)

Lay them down, these
tracks of Father, so we
who will, can follow into
the sinister light some
would call grave, others night,
Mother to those in the know.

ii (her voice)

Camels the Bedouin ride
tie the animal soul to you
who wandered far into the desert
searching for an oasis. And what
did you find but an ocean whose
shores we can stand on, thanks
to you, to see better the travesty
of time we call history. Our
footsteps in the sand will lead
others on their journeys when
home is lost. That's where
memory comes in, the door
opened on fires we build
to light our way through darkness.
Call it a place of shelter, then,
time provides in lieu of
the solace belonging brings
to wanderers like you and me.

charles bernstein

i (his voice)

I don't think I ever had
what I thought I had
going for me until
this moment it became
clear as crystal
clear as this thought
coming to me now.

ii (his voice)

counting
lines
enthusiastic
for
their
own
meaning
to
be
disclosed
I
read
(what
the
language
said)
(what's

the matter
darling
cat
got
you
hung
up)

iii (his voice)

scandal I'd gladly make
for some liberation's sake
had me climbing up the rope
of hope the world had
set on fire, so I groped
my way up or down
it no longer mattered
the way lay in tatters
I was on, then off
to the races I went
now for the sake
of assimilation of reality's
terms written as a form
of atonement for a crime
not committed so much as
translated into dust
symbolic of hist-
ory hi story

iv *miss frequency*

you point to what you want
and the clerk gives you a thumbs up

and she asks you, but you don't let her
finish, if you want the items separated
(since one of them, a piece of black-pepper chicken,
is warmed) instead you reply Just as it is, is fine
and after a long pause she combines
the items and places them all in the bag
which she then hands to you
before you leave the store
almost just as it was
before you came in

ginger murchison

— after *a scrap of linen, a bone*

In the stone compartments of flesh
is chiseled the heart's epitaph
that says, Luck made to last
will last all the way home, if
you're lucky enough to get there…

For this poet sees every springtime ruse
and then some, flowers only to be
stemmed by the tide of ice
in the veins winter is bringing as we speak.

And this wave, this current is
itself a frequency the heart knows
all too well— that well
gone to not enough, or too much for my liking. True
wit, either way, is to see past the ripple effect to
another shore, on principle foreign,
if by birth, unseen.

jennifer wallace

— after *Almost Entirely*

(her voice)

ars poetica

If I have to say yes or no,
I begrudge the answer.
Let ambiguity be the judge.

*

The more
I look
the more
I see
what is
not there.
Or is it
what isn't.

There.

*

I've bled dry the wound
I've borne, aching
to get the healing
I've needed, wet

with the blood
you were born by,
my sons, grown
bone and flesh, alive
in the making.

*

You need staying power,
I've got it.
Stay with me
and you'll go far.

It's my most famous place,
going the distance.

It stayed with me and my father
for years—the mystery
of who we were to each other,
our misunderstandings that
formed the basis of our relationship,
two identities that were never
at peace with who the other was,
let alone at peace with ourselves.

carolyn forche

i —after *What You Have Heard Is True*

(her voice)

The wars of the U.S have been perpetual,
or nearly so, and we forget that, claiming exceptionalism
as our birthright, but the powers-that-be in every generation
consolidate their position through wars and violence, and
it is the job of the poet to bear that witness, to reveal
us to ourselves and the pain we inflict upon each other.
Doing so preserves not only the truth but our humanity.
Poets tell the history of the soul, no matter how painful.
Not to do so, to bury our heads in the sand, is death
of the soul as we experience it, cutting ourselves off
from our commonwealth, our living bonds as humans.
To tap into the spirit of the language is what poets do,
thereby keeping ourselves alive to the blessing it confers.
Poetry, no, is not useful, unless imagination be used
in the telling of soul stories we can ill afford not to hear.
For that I wake up each morning and write.

ii —after *In the Lateness of the World*

(her voice)

We cringe in the face of singing to silence,
to being unheard in the cacophony out there,
nonetheless I must bring my soul to bear
upon the lines I write, or why else write?

That's why the political ramifications of
poetry reverberate in the culture now, as
it should, where the injustices we're part
and parcel of leave us no room for witness
without the empathy needed for our humanity,
for our depths out of which we're reborn,
a body at a time, in the space of language.
Give me this space is all I ask. Anything less
is propaganda, is rhetoric that destroys
the undercurrents we thrive in, wave
upon wave upon wave in the ocean of presence.

iii —after *In the Lateness of the World*

Stone calling from within, hard fate
under the pressure not of history,
nor of ethics, nor even of beauty,
but of the mystery heard beating
at the heart of the world, early or late,
spoken in silence, in the aftermath
of speech, words circling truth
and beauty, in pursuit of a myth,
of what's there that here is host of,
elegies to the unforsaken, the love
she'd husband, witnessing the age
its losses, its repose, its dark message
deciphered artfully, its language
of phlegm, cloud, sleep, ash, prayer.
Yes, here is host to what's there
by the sea, by the burning page.

marie howe

i — after *What the Living Do*

You listened to my stories you never tired
of hearing (she says to her late brother), and
gifts we gave each other word for word
assemble now in a pattern I call my own.
I would have died had I known then
what I know now. Oh, the knowledge
of secrets the least of it…

In the center was a death she mourned
and eulogized in a painting
with words, the blues awash with
the black of grief and the yellow
of gratitude, the expanse of the canvas
framed by an experience she
pronounced, again and again, as her
irrevocable foothold on the mountain
she sighted for us, a purgatory of
pain and pleasure outlasting the picture
she would paint, its outlines left
like light in a darkness so deep
she wanted to remain there, but didn't.

She made remembering a candle
that burned awhile at both ends—
to the day and to the night, where
her own two feet had taken her
as she bore her cross come time to do so,

the remembering a burning that lit
the window from within, the urn
the shape of a heart, the colors of life.

ii —after an interview w/ Joshua J. Hines

(her voice)

Time hoists me up like a flag
waving, and I let the winds
point me in the direction of
my writing, years and years
waiting before I get it all down,
but when it's done, it's done,
and I'm freed of it at last.
Time to move on, to explore
new terrain where my language
takes me, in dialogue with the dead,
as poets often are, and with the living,
with those friendships that birth
the poems one way or another,
for which I'm grateful and
indebted, that keeps me grounded
in the human sense of being
alive, being true to yourself while
others course through you,
are integral to who you are,
of time influential as a star.

dorianne laux

—after *Only As the Day Is Long*

There is an arc she follows carefully
from desire to death of desire, that runs
through the body just as it always has,
and she follows it not blindly nor
obediently but with the powers of
observation she cultivates by the earth
that gives her her direction, her voice,
and when words strike through silence
into story, she glories in the details
she gives herself to unfailingly,
working them so that they carry her,
the weight of her, into a new gravity
where the world, in its lurid majesty,
to borrow a phrase of hers, rises
where she breathes the music
of creation, the thrum of life,
the orbital path pushing and pulling her
enough times, like a heartbeat, until
she's stunned into belief,
now a raven, now a fly, now a beetle,
now an elk, now a crow, past all
unprofitable speculation, past merciless
fate we've brought upon ourselves,
upon other species, the moon opening its eye
and watching as if it's known all along,
with the stars grown dim and distant
returning like crickets in the grass,
their celestial chirping courting the sun.

carla harryman

(her voice)

The cracked open egg of an idea
posits food for the soul, all scrambled
with our assumptions about what an egg
is and why it's worth breaking it (to
make an omelet?). The chicken trying
to cross the road is there, also, reminding
us of our relationship to the other side
of the argument for or against story,
one we can't help telling and that
tells us. So we think. The question
of origins comes into it, also, whereby
we can identify with the chicken or egg
(in no particular order) or omelet served
up as a poem might be, broken lines et al.

Part Five

franz wright

(i.m. 2015)

i his voice

We weep in recognition of
what's real.
We leap in celebration of
what we feel.
We, exiled, asleep by inspiration of
day's night.
We deep in declaration of
love,
though saying so is not right,
so, we keep it locked tight.

Integration of mind
and heart is an aim
I can share, but it's
a dare others will game.
We keep them apart
—segregated they call it—
like the locker rooms in
high school—otherwise
all hell will break loose.
Dreaming mind dreams
up a storm, thinking
mind thinks up a form.
Norms of behavior follow
from the gap between them.

It's called reliable flow
and staying in the know.
I love it that way, for it
tells me just how reasonable
the world is or can be.

ii

Under the belly of lamentation
sits a tale of woe, his frustration
programmed like the telly, to earn
ratings approval by and by. He waves
to his viewers, he even saves the
bon mot or two for them, if the muse
allows. The silence that ensues
casts in relief the jokes he makes
at his own expense, laughter mixed
in with tears to make a Lazarus
of his ache. He studies the whys and
wherefores of his father's success,
a shadow that outlasts him, he thinks,
say or write what he will. So he goes
to the till daily and spends
what he doesn't have on the readers
his poems garner, prized by him as
much as they him. Everyone's happy
then for the sorrow he mines, for the
benefits accrued in his twisting lines.

iii

One has sex on the brain in a tug of war with desire
One has food on the brain because, really, why not

One has history on the brain out of respect and love for the father
One has God, that elder brother, on the brain with whom one walks hand in hand
And one has poetry, because O a broken heart burst open

iv

This man has his
father's name
to absolve him
of shame? No.
Glory glows from within
his sin.
He says:
We tattle on each
other 'cause it's fun.
We battle each other
'cause that's how it's done.
We rattle each other's
skeletons 'cause that's how
boney truth is won.
Hard asses we must be,
to play our parts
in this story.
It's all for our
art, we say,
while the palaces of
imagination get blown
apart or occupied
by whoever's got a gun.
That's how the West was won,
and the East, I bet, is in a

similar situation.
We look in each
other's eyes,
while you look away.
We play chicken
while you play,
'You don't say?'
I'd wait forever
that way.
I say: Make hay
while the sun shines.

v (his voice)

I'm here, aren't I?
Very involved in argument.

I say: Throw the book back
into the fray. Make a fracas!

Turn read into your death wish!
Turn your death-bed into a reading!

Declare our winners up to today!

Soaked in the bloodbath of history
in time for now.

Beyond control but tantalizingly watchable
is the subconscious.

Past makes present commodify the future
bought and sold in the marketplace of sound.

Alphabet soup and humble pie dished out
to the budding poets of the world won't deter
their appetite for life and glory.

Steamrolled into politics, I've discovered
depths lying beneath the pavement of stars.

Slammed against the wall of opposition, he watched
in silent protest.

He banged out a whimper of a poem in the middle
of a family holiday.

The taproot of the poet is spine plus pain, in equal measure.

The heaviness lifts with each letter written down.

Backstage in the dark wood of waiting he stood,
the thunder and rain of applause filling his ears.

I appreciate your confidence: it builds things up
that time tears down.

I told you I told you I told you that's all
I need to hear before my enemies cow me into
silence.

The solid wheel of faith keeps spinning.

People pay their respects
to the dead man walking.

Sky wonders why
it took blue so long.

Earth promises green
from the ground up.

I admit of no talent
save that of healing others
by my pain.

Soft landing after a hard
flight—what more from fancy
can one ask?

It's what we are not, that frames
what we are: a picture of frailty, pity,
and terror in the face of dying.

Born spoken for, I give myself
to death before I die. That way
I can see daily where I came from.
Truth is, the terror
makes me high.
I get off on it.
It's all I can do to look
myself square in the eye
and not say goodbye
inside the circle of my
days and nights.

Waves of its surf have
pounded my words fine as
sand that when cast ashore
say: More… More…

Spirit dying forever into
new body— this I don't
believe, but this I know.

Hungering for the unsung parts
of my soul keeps me alive.

Come, see the view
of the monster, evil
says, never letting on
the monster is you.

The ugliness I've become
is what I face
in the mirror every day.
Lord knows, I try to give
beauty a fair shake
by what I make.

In the face of death
every conscious breath
is a koan
on loan from
the precipice.

I've sold out everything
except my soul: she keeps
me whole.
The color of death stains
her not, but paints
me into a corner from
which I can see my world
as the ring I stepped into
all those years ago, in which
I plan to leave my carcass
not my fire, the heat of which
you, dear reader, can take with

you to help, if it would,
warm up your cold spells by,
that I saw reflected
in the moon from my bed
at night, my beloved
beside me in its light,
neither cold nor hot
but re-mixing what I am
with what I'm not.

It wants to win,
this ticker of mine,
each beat of the way
toward doom, that
I be lost in a bigger room
of your dwelling, Lord,
as in a womb.

At least have the decency, Lord,
to put my clothes back on,
unlike my lover that sits
naked at the edge of the bed
with me now.

vi —after his final interview, w/ Sarah Messer

(his voice)

Time for me is measured in beats,
line by line opening space,
it's the only way I can experience
poetry as I know it, or feel it,
bearing down on my soul until

I free myself of it by writing it,
by surrendering to the muse or
whatever, I can't find words otherwise,
the words come to me as I yield
to them, it is a gift to oneself
to let the words in, to welcome
the resentments, the fears, the angers
that propel the poem's shape
and give the lines their measure,
which is what I experience as music,
always and first as music. Happy
and alone deep in poetry's spaces,
which I can't find words for but
keeps me on track, realizations
I live for through language, that
is the source of a poet's happiness,
no matter the price paid, shadows
in a dream that we all are in this world.

harryette mullen

—after *Urban Tumbleweed*

Urban tumbleweed, she calls herself,
flowing into nature to have an
influence, an impact on the passing
scene, the vale of tears in which
she'd make a 'soul,' valued in the
act of making, contracting and expanding
in the City, in accordance with laws of the tumbleweed,
aka laws of the wind—

jane hirshfield

i (her voice)

I would have my poetry declared
permanent assays into impermanence,
were I fortunate to be occasionally read
and remembered, lines of my heart
stretched taut, web-like, the spider's art
finely detailing the everyday expanse
I've hiked, stepping across it as only
the poet can, luck turning to chance
turning to fate, or is it to peace with one's dead
spoken through silences we inhabit, home
I return to, sky measured by leaves of grass
earth gifts me, the length of my passing name
a note in the universal song called time.

ii

For she darts in and out of the caverns
of her own mind, to find the turns
of phrase she needs for the poems
she writes, that write her into existence,

posing the question, how far or high…?
its answer the latitude we give ourselves
as to the rainbow in the ephemeral sky
as it lands and imprints the heart,
butterfly-like, before beating on.

iii — after *Ledger*

(her voice)

The demise of the planet is nigh upon us
and writers, if they don't cave, sing a chorus
of warnings I aim to be a part of, god forgive us.
Yes, you can't live without the fondnesses of the heart
but the darknesses of the earth you feel entering the bloodstream
of our daily life harden the most faithful of us.
Still, we resolve to limit the damage as far as we are able,
to treasure those moments the trees wave to us
and the sky, if not widens the view, measures it
against our mirroring eye.

iv —after *Ledger*

The bowels emptied, the bile
duct working overtime, its role
essential, a lifeline to the intestine
from the liver's acids, to drain
the yellowish-green fluid and
break down fats, nothing bland
about it, a curious flow of salts
and cholesterol and water that jolts
the reader to a difficult reckoning,
isn't that what poets do: sing
the fierce fables of our time
for what we lack: clear understanding
and new words for the sublime.
So, she forges ahead, listening
to Earth's human-sized counsel,
were it possessed of a soul,

were it found to be useful,
were it heard above the steady din
of a darkening, swerving rain
after long drought, sorrow drained.

mark doty

—after *What Is the Grass: Walt Whitman in My Life*

(his voice)

I am palpable in my praise of the poet,
the one I read trying to encompass
his expansive spirit, his cosmic imprint
of human, body and soul, in his pages,
the ones he called 'Leaves of Grass'
and which continue to grow and blossom
so many years hence, a parcel of the eternal
held in place by language we barely
wrap our minds around, language heated
to a temperature forged from depths
and heights that only poetry can embody,
in all its strangeness and daring, fully
alive, and yet unconstrained by the body,
loosed by imagination ecstatic to calm,
singular to plural, essential to structural,
limitless energy radiantly transforming
from sensation to sensation, as power
open at the root of existence, of time
and space and beyond, sweeping into voice,
the speaker at the pinnacle of his realization,
continuous, promised, momentous, seen
as only the self, in the other, is seen,
and heard, too, in the expression of love
that he brought forth from the source
that held him, vital, true, mysterious,
and, for all that, American.

tony hoagland

i

The portentous poet making unpretentious
use of his poetry to skewer the world around
and inside him, his heartfelt sighs disguised
or supplanted by the historical tides he swims
in, every passing moment, to the shore
he'd give anything to stay on, replete with house,
two kids, wife and a dog greeting him on its
hind legs as he returns home at night, tired
but certain no life is better than this one.

Instead, he swims further and further out
each time, on waves his imagination
conjures and to which, as metaphor, he harnesses
himself, a lifeline to keep him afloat, buoyed
by words he can't get enough of, by that sea
of language that knows no bounds, no end.

ii book of mourning

In his book of mourning for a dying
America, in which he offers prayers
heavenward that sound out hell,
he had themes that someday
would come to fruition—rage, anger,
loneliness, unhappiness, theft, guilt,
bitterness, self-pity, absence of love,
entitlement—they were all there,

powering their way up through words
to the plot ruminating of his story
that was yet to be written, an epic
voyage taking its sweet time to reach
its destination, a mystery that would
never be solved while he was alive,
since the clues lay buried in the back
of his mind while the daily rounds
left his heart in his mouth, there
for all to see, someday, and hear
cover to cover, read on the fly,
spiritually speaking, crossing over
again and again hoping to die.

kim addonizio

i after a poem of hers

(her voice)

In the bottomlessness of grief, I found my voice
and have never looked back its darkness my light
my guide my way forward into the horizons
tumbling out of the present like shards I'll sweep
up by the broom of my poem and maybe then put
myself back together if my words have any say.

ii after a poem of hers

(her voice)

I have ho-ed my way through
the blues and back again, and still
the Negritude is a labor of fun
and disease and intoxication I
have gotten down on, though no tease, I—
more a shared mesmerizing I've ridden
bars and saloons on, to fear and beyond.
I swear I've never seen as many
ghosts haunting a place between sets
as in a blues joint—swarming to be near
the music till the sun comes up,
all night long dancing and drinking
the cobwebs in their skulls away,
the stage their Mecca of rebirth.

sarah arvio

i (her voice)

I was going to admit
this was narcissistic twaddle,
with the bone tied to eternities
aimed for from within.
While outside the weather
fooled us, as we put in
our appearances, as we
said our hellos and goodbyes.
We fled the corners for
a look at, or in, the center
where we wed the lines,
one after the other, that led
to meaning. No story,
mind you, other than mine.

ii (her voice)

The trick is in curling up into a ball
and letting the pen point you in the
direction of the voice or voices you
hear, it's not automatic so much as
manual shift—either way, you get
to a place you didn't know was there.

What's your aggression for?
What's your now about?

iii (her voice)

There have been others
I won't say who
or how many
There have been many
others who can say
about me what I can't
say about myself,
And for that I cannot
thank them enough,
nor forgive myself.

iv —after *Cry Back My Sea*

It's for all suffering lovers, she says,
an oxymoron if ever there was one.
Then she wades in deep in her sea
of grief and wit, and her sea, wave
upon wave, responds, not in kind,
her unkindness would show, but
in spades, a blackened heart no more
black than white, a colorful heart
read with amour, armored all the same,
game she is, for love and war for all
they're worth, and worthy of the name,
the trauma of her past has a new
atlas, at last, the tree of her heart's
growth splayed across a sky of routes
she's traveled the stormy length of,
the aftermath's calm her recollection's balm.
Tiller of her heart's garden now, for
tall tales out of spaded soil rich with the soul
of hurt, softened by where it's been and will go,
what its leafiness and veininess go to show.

jesse glass

(his voice)

It behooves one to know who one is
but truth is elusive when it comes to
pathological and poetical too. Who
we are eluding us when true and false
are played fast and loose with. Who
knows anything, really, when persona
loses its grip in corresponding reality.
Who am I to judge, except for what
I see and hear and taste and feel,
a haptic tactic my brain relies on
bodily. We poets stick to these facts
mainly, but ideas do come to the fore
We'll see what the future brings.
For now, we sing. That's what poets are for:

Hamlin is the Piper's digs
where they confuse rats for pigs
The snouts that forage in the trash
end up gilding dross with ash.
We poets pipe our Beauties
in this way, as ceiling's Tutties
look down upon us from above
and pipe their notes of Love.

Time will test this poet's theory
of space infinitely poetic.
In the meantime, I'll wax

and wane with the voice erotic
which shocks, being as politic
as it is gnomic.

vijay seshadri

i (his voice)

History's slave, not of of
but of with, takes love
apart and puts it back
together again, a sack
of magical thinking
done with, eschewing linking
arm in arm with space-time's
spins, for homeless rhymes
heard on the run, from
there to here, a hum-
dinger of a gesture, free will's
in all but name, that wheels
the sovereign I into a You
you will succumb to,
manned up, and up,
under story's whip.

ii

He splits the world in two: what he can
have of it and what he can afford to give
away. The tight accounting of a man
shows what he's worth, whether to love
him or not is the question he'll leave
you with. It's up to you, reader, to plan
accordingly: either way the earth will live.

iii (his voice)

We arrange the rationale to fit the denial
of what it would describe, in feeling
the emotion that lands us back in
the body we never left to begin with,
save when the idea of it overwhelmed
us and cast us one wave at a time onto
a shore we didn't expect, were afraid of
not seeing, on the journey embarked upon
precisely because we felt the absence
taking us there that no song could utter.
We witness the arrival as another departure
were we able to hear the sound of waves
sibilant as syllables driving us there, but
understanding the destination as provisional
as a body in time, a spirit in space, ambivalent
in the end about Abstraction having its say.

iv Seshadri's Eliot

He loops sentences out of his psychic damage,
what later they'd call The Modern Age.
He refuses the peach but extends his reach
into terrain where his roots and notes flourish
in the soil of violence, yet is squeamish
and tormented as he prods the beach,
removing quotation marks from around the Sun
and dissolving the Self's music just for fun.
The open road swerved through the rock,
not past it, while his path opens a crack
in the seams of experience human and god-like
where one's voice embodies, were thunder to speak,

the fearful divine. And shines a starry speck.
(You were right, he thinks, and so utterly unheroic.)

v —after *That Was Now, This is Then*

One poet writing to another,
living or dead, bespeaks a continuum
we would do well to consider
existing in the service of none other
than a change of paradigm long overdue,
how when the greatest living
are the least dead among us, we revel
in what they reveal about the need
most in ourselves to hear again
in the here and now no revolution
in the blood but the evolving
body-invested mind at play
in the fields of the world
as it migrates between
provocations and devotions
and we meet each other…halfway…for it's not
the truth of the times so much as
the music of the times we're after,
a tune not to go to sleep by
(I've stopped that god-awful music at least)
but one to consider our life by, our life
while we're still living it,
accompanied, live.

jennifer barber

—after *Rigging the Wind*

It is no wave that carries
her out to sea, for the shore
knows its kind, the cool breeze
blowing over the sand *–how hot is the sand?—*
she feels with her fingers—*how cold is the water?—*
but not every surface heats up the same way.
She knows where the wind
comes from, what makes
the air move.
It starts with the sun.

But there is no shore,
there is no sea.

She binds
the pieces of this landscape
with a touch
her words have,
heavy
with light.

gregory dunne

i (his voice)

The poet washes down his wishes with
sake I can taste on my lips down to my gut,
that's what poetry can do, or has done
for me, yet we mustn't scrimp on the mystery
of it all, either, but who am I to say?
The days and nights I've spent writing
have helped me survive this world, and for
that I'll always be grateful to poetry.
Shame we can't all have a name to go
with it in the annals we declare. Throw
the bait in the waters and watch the carp
swim up from the depths, is the lesson
I've learned, myself among them here.
Watch how the ripple effect on the surface
of things becomes a tide heading for shore
in a sea of anonymity we all must navigate.
Japan is my home away from home
the way a poem is, for some, their fate.
I'll go the distance with anyone for a taste
of fame. To wit, anything else is a waste
of time and effort, is the motto I live by,
if not dream by, come hell or high water.

ii —after *Other/Wise*

Sentimental does not do justice to the sentiment
he wraps himself in, to fold into himself the moment

he comes to see and feel, the heart of the evidence
the world presents, time after time, as providence,
divine or otherwise, for such carnal happiness
as courts its own extinction, thrown away to bless
whatever comes after, not seeking abundance
so much as fortitude and faith to bear witness
to the higher being in himself, the dance
that the others he loves moves to, from emptiness
all the way to the decision he obeys, not continuance
but the oath he swears by, deep down, win or lose.

mary karr

— after *Venom Rum*

Each farewell felt in the bone
for the finishing ash to come,
now held in language soaked
to the core, the needle sewn
by a hand crafty, mutilated
with the sores earned crosswise,
borne goodbye upon goodbye,
until layers stitched as cloth
worn, draped over the body
laid out on the stone, forlorn,
bereft of breath, entombed
in a world no worse for what
passes for wear, her wherewithal
worded into one lifeline after
another, a visible light poured
out of sounds of all that's hidden,
but she knows how to listen,
in spite of herself, in spite,
which, once heard, you can't unhear,
milk or venom, the choice hers,
and, reader now taught, ours.

john brehm

— after *Help Is on the Way*

(his voice)

A vehicle enters the highway, its front hood
covered with birds flying off every which way.

*

She glides into a space
to fill it with her grace.
How could I know her
before I found her
turning away her telling face.

*

Fishermen arrive by dust of waves
the fish swim through, whose mouths
are hooked by gravity pulling them along,
eyes opened to the spectacle of you
holding on to the rod for dear life.

*

Between the fool's gold and
the beggar's choice lies
the vastness of earthly human
desire, because I felt it

and then woke up:
whoever said I was who
I said I was.

*

Nothing made sense
into the burnished days
of my emptiness
though I tried
to give it shape,
though I strove
to take heed
as the wind
had warned me to do.

After all the words
spoken and unspoken
there's nothing that isn't
written in the wind,
I came to learn,
and nothing new
to teach.

Let the hand
crossing this page
feel its age and pause
before understanding comes,
past cursing, to the one
who writes it down,
for whom time now
is full
of places the wind
won't touch.

hiromi ito

—on a poem of hers

(her voice)

In this age of ash and diminishment
shall I speak, shall I utter my displacement
onto other things and sing, before abandonment
overtakes my voice of what we were meant to be?
I cannot say what words suffice any more
but the sound of my loneliness lifts the lid
off the box I'm in, and I scatter to the four winds
all that I had hoped to say, and leave it to you
who read this to answer, "Where are you from?"
with, "Back home."

forrest gander

i (his voice)

I stopped counting the days
since you left this earth,
but the pain accompanies me
to every new arrival, every
new awakening presaged by
the wanderer with a story
to tell, were anyone listening,
prejudged by the oracular
vision I've let go, released
to the dust I settle in, where
the outline of your body is
visible to one who will not
stop counting the ways.

ii

I remember the power emanating
from your presence at a reading
you gave in Tokyo. Then, years
later, on another visit, you appeared
fragile from deep loss, yet still
resonating with authentic tenderness.
And I felt, on an altogether
different continuum: Outside
you separate the men from the boys.
Inside they're
one and the same.

iii —after *Be With*

(his voice)

Have I been forgiven?
for being strong enough to face inevitability
but too weak to die.
Have I been accepted?
for being who I am, against
the grain of history making.
Have I been truthful?
in spite of myself, to
the revelations of love.
Have I been here?
when there was all I
could fall into, until now.

michael sowder

(his voice)

Endless rounds of
do-nothing battles…
Everybody's agendas are
up against one another's
in life's everyday spheres
but coming here to India
and devoting time & effort
to meditating has opened my eyes.
Here the ties are released
and the new balance you need
raises you onto a higher plane
of being that touches on why
we're all here, not just
the me myself. All of us can hear
a voice calling on occasion, but here
I allow myself to hear it full throttle,
the hum of the universe that
makes the divine music of the spheres.
Here I can hear with fewer distractions
each note of the endless harmony
as it rises, and I learn how to face
it and accept it and the whoosh
of space and time colliding accelerates
into a cosmic spin I can see myself
floating in. Mush, some call it.
Fair enough. Till next time…
Whatever attracts us reminds
us of a debt we have yet to repay.

diane seuss

i (during the coronavirus pandemic)

Harm's way we're in won't
put the brakes on my life
which is mine to live, over
sixty be damned! I have
paid my dues, weathered
strife and woe to get here,
and I swear by poetry no
more, for it's only more life
I want, no matter the price.
Let the ice in my veins
congeal some other day!

ii —on a poem of hers

She cleaves to clarity, certain
it will save her from herself
at this late stage in her life,
one in which clarity shines
down on all the good it does
her, not remembering what
happened so much as making
happen a remembering, a storyline
to take her to a present full
of anonymous pleasures she
would trade nothing for, not
even the poem called a sonnet
which she writes to hold back

The Forgetting she knows all
too well will come, when the time
comes, to take her home. Until
then she flashes her goods
and relishes even the bad she did,
remembering it with a laugh
and a tear, no stranger to herself,
a trick of the contradictions
she makes much of, played
on a bandwidth she calls her own,
its sounding a shimmering.

claudia emerson

She enters form by its back door
and freeze-frames its unfolding
like pictures on a wall, no story
save the one heading for the exit
as she speaks, the door behind her
closed tight, leaving it untold.

li-young lee

(his voice)

Angers have driven my soul to points
hidden in the east-west matrix where
convulsions led me to writing
poems and throwing caution to the wind
that sweeps up talent and terror alike.
What I've seen constitutes a mirage
you would swear was real, and around
its edges I encamped for years on end.
Now the truth comes out in the music
my heart beats to, a rhythm no self
can claim, shores swept by unending
waves of bliss, waves of unending
mind I take up residence in, whose
thoughts return me to a storied death I own.

nikky finney

Queenly inquiring of the issues of the day
and night, her poetry implicating like a knife
the injustices she calls out and comes to
correct, at least on the page where words
make things happen that otherwise would
not, she avows her calling in practical ways
of the world, the one she lives in and dies
for, believing underneath the darkness is
a light resurrecting the moments earth
has made the sun for, a golden girl
free and clear making her way home.

joseph harrison

—after *Sometimes I Dream That I Am Not Walt Whitman*

the ventriloquist's song (his voice)

I've sung 'soul' so many times the whole
idea of it, fanciful or real, is a solo riff on
sound and sense commiserating as twin
undercurrents to the muse I give my all
to, rhyming here and there in perfect
unison with the flow I harbor, affect
plumbed, for the next oceanic swell
carrying me aloft and leaving me a shell
of myself, the one I put my ear to,
that I might hear the whole day through,
night notwithstanding, the dream font
in which I, baptized anew, nonchalant
and poised, can reinterpret the signs
and read them, all told, between the lines,
my voice lingering in the air, angelic,
apropos, echoing the tradition's relic
remixed in a collaboration of passion,
purpose and ongoing allusion.

sophie cabot black

—after *The Exchange*

the poetry read with each line a summons
to its own undoing, meanings a holding
back from some rendezvous, a withholding
of information necessary for the coming
exchange, near or far, required of us who
participate in the formation of selves
exhumed, though still pulsing with energy
and life, from our bodies, that lie
under the stories waiting to be told
again, veering away from any endings
but this one, clear, ominous, borne.

michael s. collins

i

The fire instigator folds his matchsticks
into lines that, for some, are a lonely fix
for the dreaded history one seeks to escape,
his every last syllable by its suspect shape
trying to give first things a certainty and sheen
we, but for him, won't otherwise have seen
while he hears his muse, strong,
saying in words that (safely) belong :

poet, the balls you'll need
have failed other men so
be on the lookout, the walls
are crawling with vipers,
nests of them that'll come
crawling out one by one.
It's no use pretending
they're not there. Facing
your fears is what this is
all about, but years can
wear a man down, so be
careful, I'll be there for
you when the time comes.

ii —after a poem of his

"this secret song from the soil / left hidden under my skin"
—Yusef Komunyakaa

The voice, or the tone of it,
sounds familiar. The anger
submerged in rage immersed in
fear you won't give in to,
the violence provoked in
your mind—or is it brain—
as you look back
on that day's event, stuck
on replay for as long as words
speak, for as long as words say:
Kill the seed, kill the unborn
hope buried in the ground,
nip any sprout in the bud
of the living part that dreams,
channels the voices you hear,
gives expression to the mysteries
you'd celebrate, if you could,
before it retreats underground
once again as—the poet says—
this secret song from the soil
which we hear every day,
to rise again another day.

nick flynn

— after a web interview w/ Kaveh Akbar

(his voice)

After the addition of a subtracted
life to the poem, what have
you got? A recovering addict
holding on for dear life—to
those precious lifelines one
can't think of living without.
So, I go my own way in the poem
where I meet up with my recovering
self, and listen in on the ensuing
dialogue. What have I learned?
What have I had to sacrifice? What
notions of safety have had to slide
away, where risk can enter and
a pulse be felt? A heartbeat of
desire's body, weightless in
open space, a tell-tale narrative
of, when all is said and done, grace.

bob hicok

(his voice)

Changes? I'm like WTF?
A comfort zone that's pure and simple.
Perfect. I am made in my maker's image.
Gaming the protectors.
I'm an indulgent game freak.
Swizzle stick for the man with money.
I say a prayer for the little people.
Inspire me, poets, though we know
they won't.
Hard-scrabble life with no pot
to piss in is not for me.
Yeah. Cruelty aside, I'm like that.

kwame dawes

He would be stone,
hardened against the
gloom, obituaries, bones,
dust, grieving, tomb,
emptiness, rot, dead,
blood, stink, anomie—
yet as prophet of forgiveness
takes it all in, bliss
of his brokenness, of his shadow
written on every exit home.

Part Six

claudia rankine

— after *Citizen: An American Lyric*

(her voice)

The second person you are
is first and foremost other
than who you think you are, I
submit, so that we may see
better what can open us up,
momentarily, to new understanding, of what our stories
told mean to us when a speaker
can claim all pronouns as hers,
or his, collective stories
settled into inside the body,
coming to me, pulled
in from the racialized spirit
of the times, being present,
then coming out, for everybody's
story, a citizen lyric,
without having to ask
whatever happened to the woman
who said that?

layli long soldier

i —on a poem of hers

She cancels the debt of loss
by living into it, and settling
there, on her knees.
How else take the wind
at your back and hold on.

ii —after *Whereas*

Not erased nor cancelled
out but her style of speaking
from star to bone instills
the capacity to respond
The great outdoors the grasses
language rich as she is
pour the words out like water
to heal the wounds a deep practice
for powers' sake for engaging new terms
as the stigma of genocide deforms
the trying effort at speech the poem
a tired artifact already different from
its identity native to defiance
The piecemeal shared with wholeness
a mixed message she delivers considering
that it is a dish served tasted in the blood
a table sat at prayed at spoken at
in a room the poet makes her own
boundaries her own land her own
even the circular disclaimer her own.

d.a. powell

— after a radio interview

(his voice)

This over-the-airwave hustle
will land me in store-bought
terrain I've been years approaching
and at the same time distancing myself
from, eeny-meeny-miny-moe-ing my way
to a deeper drill for the real goods that'll
stand out for standing up for action I'll not
wager less on but more and more, dangers
included, especially those that put one in harm's
way when reaching out, where we all need
to be, a freedom-shout poets like me make,
a sky-ing lift we seek for breaking new ground
to stand on, on our own, alone here together.

lee ann roripaugh

— after *Year of the Snake*

Glimpsed by its intricate particulars, and
insinuating she's had enough experience,
her animal life beguiles and bewitches
to the extreme
limit of desire she deftly stokes
like a furnace in winter's bone.
The crushing, the cutting, the molting all
reconfigure not so much the self
as the other whom she would devour, her mouth wide
open, snake-like in the middle
of striking its prey, being dangerous
her ploy to survive the seasonal
return of so much that gets left behind
delicately wrapped in a shroud of words
woven out of her creatureliness,
her scandalous breath.

matthew olzmann

—after "Letter to Someone Living Fifty Years from Now"

Ladies and gentlemen, we have made a fuss
like the frog that's taken up residence in the garden
bellowing his song in the night air. We have
sought dispensations where jealousy fuels the ranks
and the leader reserves the right to strike first.
I've tried to sell merchandise with my name
on it, earmarked for ostensible wisdom. Likewise
merriment of mine indexed the stars, one sky
at a time, until the sad constellations spoke.
I was trouble, troubled by the age.
We readied ourselves for speech
that never came. I was ruled by contingency
and risk but couldn't keep my secrets.
For if I have learned anything, I have learned
that if history is written by the winners,
the losers—forgive me—write poetry
all day and all night, their root cause
one of beauty in time for all that's lost
but found in the sound the words make,
making their lines echo you who come after.

steven b. herrmann

— after *Spiritual Democracy*

i (his voice)

A bit of the toughening needed.
Storm-tossed psyche must
have its hatches battened down
against wave after wave of
possibly fatal destructive forces.
My job is to show the
leatherstockings how to survive
out there. Somebody's got to do it.
And I'm just the man to do it, too!

It's a foregone conclusion that
when mapping this frontier of
the psyche, some pioneers will
lose their way, and some may even
drown. My way has sunlight and
brightness working for it, in a
sky others have navigated by the
stars. But those preceding me
accompany me in spirit. I cannot
here name them all; a few will do
whose names history already
resonates with. A winner-take-all
scenario, I'm afraid. But then, what
isn't? Darwin has by rights the
theoretical model cornered here

in the west. The east won't even
merit a footnote. Welcome to the bigs
of the west, the rest is rigged with bliss.

Smile the smile of surrender and
you're doomed to be torn asunder.
Mark the words of one who has seen
ships wrecked out at sea, never
to return. There's a certain certainty
in life, spelled e-v-i-l, a root source
of much of the human comedy or
tragedy, call it what you will. It's
still got us in its sights, and we all
must know (or learn) how to survive
its onslaught when it comes. And
it will come... We're the heavy hitters
here. Learn from us.

We critics have a nose, too, for treasures
down in the deeps, but rarely risk
anything more than the bends.

Garden Productions presents
A Calamity Film starring
the mega-stars and losers
of the 19th & early 20th centuries.
We're no gap-inducing society
but we find and power
over the gaps without compunction,
crack shots we are, too. Our
power borrowed goes a long way.

So long, suckers… Sorry we can't
stay longer, but the way forward's
not in waiting, and we're ready
and willing. Call me pumped.

The starry way may be viable
for a start. But the long haul
needs powering. Always has,
always will.

ilyse kusnetz

i (i.m.) (her voice)

Come and see me happen
There's no telling how much
longer I have

I'm losing him
Our time with our beloved
on earth is a blessing,
and we may accept it as a given,
the blessing of love,
that makes for consolation,
that points toward immortality,
our consciousness in a way
uploaded into the universe.

Mine because I've sat down

He understands under the surface

Dear voices he hears coming through
loud and clear,

The foot in the door to the cosmos
is a magic mirror of sorts

ii (her voice)

I waited
for those moments

to come
but they never did
unless waiting was
the death I feared
would take me away
from you for good.
Even so, I waited,
knowing I would leave
the moments behind
that we made together,
those pockets of time
that carried us along
into the dark, where I now
am, no longer waiting.

iii —after *Angel Bones*

(her voice)

I will never not speak again
of all that we have been
to each other, without even knowing it,
and by speaking, let show
the bond we once had,
that tied us to the trail of events
leading us out of ourselves
into the mystery we both marvel at.
I will never not feel again
what we once were to each other,
the pain, the laughter, the thrill
of it not gone, but like a child's balloon
floating up into the sky
as far as the eye can see.

paisley rekdal

— after *Nightingale*

Immersed in wild energy, she steers
her way from pain to pain to ascertain
not limits so much as parameters at
a depth where humanness ventures into
godedness, the immortals she read about
when a child trying to fathom her father's
sacrifice, her mother's artifice. She unpools
the light at the foot of her memory, to cut
her way through what darkness, embodied,
dares, horror upon horror looked at unblinking,
change clothed for a turning in or out
one body at a time, of desire's reach
surpassingly familiar in its burning,
its heat of want, as she, woman of words
and loss, is given to mourning in a language
of violence endured for which there are
no words, no descent adequate to the experience
of it, felt in the flesh of time, yet she seeking
redress in the afterlife of space, spirit's
womb, or is it lyric's wound, or the song
at the end of song where imagination
opens the I to loss and all it demands
from the memory that won't let go,
that won't be there again—
her severalty of self amid
the soughing of the trees.

natasha trethewey

(her voice)

—after an op-ed in *The New York Times* 2020

Why am I so happy
I'm not taking a selfie
in the casket, loss of personal
peace in the time of a pandemic
notwithstanding?
Okay, Badge, quit your cruelty
and violence against
my people and I'll raise higher
hopes for us All, in our beloved nation.
Give and take in the battle for justice
goes on apace in the country of my childhood.
You don't get it if you think it's ever over with,
the scars, the slights, the symbols of white supremacy,
though now it's hard to believe they're coming
down and I don't mean just statues and flags, I mean
mindsets entrenched in centuries of racism and
injustice, they're coming down and, in their place,
will be erected perhaps a nobler version of
ourselves for which I'll fight until my 'dying day,'
a day that came to my ancestors often by the end
of a rope, or the threat of one, but today we celebrate
as Independence Day, a light indispensable
in the darkness, like my mother was for me
as a child growing up in Mississippi, as I keep
it tight with you, America.

craig arnold

i.m., lost in Yakushima, Japan April 27, 2009

The infiltrating tourist-poet, footloose
in Japan, gone too soon, lost to
the mountaintop volcano he visited
in the south, the seeker of movement,
excitement and danger. He took his
chances climbing, he made a name
for himself rhyming. A story he lived
but never quite finished, or at least not
on a grace note, anyway. Instead, lost
one night near the summit, never to
come back down the slope again, alive.
He's part of other people's unfinished
stories now, they recount moments
or sing of passing encounters with this
poet. He snapped the book shut on his story.
Now we must remember him. His last
day alive he fell in love
with an edge or ledge he never saw.

mari l'esperance

i (her voice)

As long as there are boundaries
to be negotiated between
sacred and profane, shamans will exist.
Where these boundaries fall, of course,
vary from culture to culture.

*

Dead white men rule the domain
of poetry. To ride their coattails
is a breeze. It's a way to score
brownie points in a world that's
indifferent to girls with ambition.
That's me, and the male club
I want in on hardly notices me.
But, Honey, this bee has a sting she
knows how to use, with digs in
all the right places. Time & fortune's
on my side, but this waiting game's
unendurable.

ii (her voice)

You wanna watch fire
grow, not grass?
You wanna feel the
stampede of the instincts

in the blood?
You wanna primal energy
at zero remove?
Human beings wouldn't
know what to do with it,
except pervert it into
conflict and war,
engaging in disputes over
the size of the penis
or who gets a bigger hearing…

*

Feeling? It's how you
function as a poet.

The expression "Keep
somebody in your thoughts"
is no misnomer. Our thoughts
can and do change reality

as certain people vibrate & resonate together…

nadine sabra meyer

—on reading some of her poems

Just knowing there are good poems
being written out there helps take
some of the edge off the bite of things,
knowing there are souls locked in mortal
combat with themselves or with the world,
those for whom a word or a line in a poem
is a matter of life and death— it gives one
pause in the flux and flotsam of existence,
and calms one's breathing to a slow
and steady heartbeat in the adoring emptiness.

faith shearin

I like what she does
with the ordinary:
she dances with it,
and the air around it glows.
What is it about West Virginia poets
who tell it like it is? Who
speak the world back
into view before the words
for it fall, silent.

anis shivani

Now we're talking about the teeth
of History, devouring everything in its path.

The passerby interviewed:
So, what's your assessment of the damage?

*

I was thinking the worst of you, History,
but have managed to find use for you
despite it all.

*

He beautifies the historical
imperative to death (one of his critics insinuates), until what's
left is timeless ease in its absence,
a decadent lounging in the corridors
of power where truth is an echoing
footfall distantly heard.

victoria chang

— after *Obit*

(her voice)

I have died countless times to live
more deeply in this world, to give
back what was gifted to me by
my parents, and their parents before
them. So, I write my way back to
where I am alive, feeling my way
into the mess of things again, loss
being what I must reconcile somehow,
letting go being what makes us whole
again, after being split apart by grief.
I have died countless times to live
is my mantra now, and will be my
word-pillar I cling to in times of
future loss, which we know will come,
say or do what we will. Each poem
I wrote helped me re-wire my brain
and put it more in sync with my heart,
so much dying in which to deepen
my experience of what I have to give.
Please, I tell myself, don't stop
learning from your losses, be less
embittered by the remnants you're left with.

rigoberto gonzalez

—after *So Often the Pitcher Goes to Water until It Breaks*

Darkness he writes about,
bone deep, opens pathways
in the soul, of doubt
that his certainties appraise.

Pigs, dogs, butterflies,
bulls, the dead, or their names,
shadowing the lit pages strewn
with paths into and out of
more than memory, that maggots
feed on, the long mourning after.

Corpse, cemetery, coffin, hearse, undertaker—
over and over proliferating like rabbits—
but the rooster crowing about it all,
you, like the bloom of dawn.

Ash congealing into flesh—
darkness awakening on the tongue—
shrouds loosening into words—
secrecies of the body told
by a stone screen
on which is shown
your I, or its image.

What you look at, what you focus on,
'only to see how far you've gotten'—

not past the border but inside it,
where it hurts to envision home,
where home is imagining of pain,
where pain is the task of eyes
to see, or its cost, accusingly, clearly.

If it's true then, it's true
now, death's emptiness
being poured out of the body,
until the moment
when you're held
in the darkening, translucent light
of a star.

stephanie burt

— after *The Poem Is You*

(her voice)

You won't find 100% white label here.
We mingle in the American mix
to make sense, or try to, of the many
in one we aspire to be, to marvel at
the varied nature of the beast we
claim as our own, beauty et al,
and to remark on what makes us tick
far from the clockwork ordering we love.

kazim ali

(his voice)

Tamarin, we bond by bodies
but build by embodied words,
the bounty of love, ambition
and balance. Those energies
we keep in our wheel of karma,
come what will. We sacrifice
for who we want to be, giving
all we are, the only star we can
follow righteously in a nation
where we are denied by the
color of our skin the inalienable
rights guaranteed by our
Constitution, though it is my
belief, my mission to say the
divine right of poets supersedes
that of kings—always has, always
will. Put that in your wheel
and stoke it, whydon'tya?!

jeffrey angles

(his voice)

The weirdness of poets baffles the mind.
Seer added to the mix is a gold mine
of riches more embarrassing than a clear
sign when none is called for. We wave
to one another across a chasm narrowing
with the years, and many have passed,
it's true, which I'm feeling now more than ever.
The bones we carry, the flesh we marry,
the spirit buries in its quest for transcendence.
But who can say if clay we end up as
doesn't have the last word, as my salt of
the earth grandma of a gay guy can tell you.
The fairness of the world unwinds into oblivion
for us all, or most of us. But I won't look any gift
horse in the mouth on my watch. What happens
to me each step of the way, I bow to.
There is no how-to for success, I've learned,
only accidents and luck, not who you bed,
the well-fed among us notwithstanding.
Connecting over time gives us space
to be revealed, again and again, with conjugal
ties and lies thrown into the bargain.
I tread the streets of the City with glee,
and with stress I'd add,
what wherewithal I have, gleaned from my Dad
who taught me to teach myself, and more.
One whom I've partnered grants wholeness

to my life. So let strife dissolve, I pray,
into new boundaries that expand and contract
for the perpetual birth I now see is possible.
This taproot, however, is no match
for the coin of the realm we moderns
hew to, and yet the ancient eye one
sees with brings us to new places
in our lives I can't deny, a
smoking hot transformation
at every turn. Would that we could
burn at this pace and seize the heat
as our own. Embers in a snowfall
is all we glean in our daily lives, the
fallout of a thousand years of learning
that we have no choice but to uphold
as the way forward, no backward-
churning waters for us. So onward,
though slow we will go.

carmen gimenez smith

She knocks the idols off their pillars
and joins the revolution starting now
Where will she go how will she know
She has no truck with the status quo
yet questions what will replace it
It's a man's world through and through
she says and she'll make peace some
other time for the sake of the kids
who have to live in it, say what she will.

amy king

(her voice)

I say the way forward my way,
not for the sake of words per se, nor
for poets I praise, but for power
I embrace as the sunlit day is mine
to husband as I please, no bride
to a fickle muse. It's the line
I use to get me where I need to
go, onward on the back of each
sentence spoken, each universe
revised in the going, parallel or not.
All the rest—yes— is rot.

Part Seven

john murillo

—after *Kontemporary Amerikan Poetry*

The climate, memory, changes the terrain
clasped close as the weight of his pain
carried in words he deploys, a slow train
of thought, a meandering, dull bloodstain
that isn't there, but is, his rhythm humane
and bluesy, his plot winding, serpentine,
his diction drenched in fight or flight
which he chooses in the darkness of night,
street paved with sonnets his cred now,
their fourteen-lined rage showing how
one's forebears, who put themselves
on the line, expect one to do the same,
their prosody offering trenchant clues
to one's dreaming, lyric by any other name.

tracy k. smith

— after *Life on Mars*

The great Maybe she explodes wide open
as per Big Bang, though with a qualifying 'could be'
strung between the erotic Yes and the platonic Know
that lasts for the entirety of time she will admit,
careful of the historical spaces that would engulf
the unsuspecting psychonaut as she traverses
the universe of pleasure and pain, the human
expanse that, black-hole-like, collapses in
on itself until the underworld is all there is,
not believed in exactly but with shoulder chipped
by history—whose isn't?—a place she carries
like a mountain of weight she'd arrive at, words
gleaming far-off yet spoken true, were her path
trustworthy, cautiously taken in pursuit of the dead
who, after a lifetime in the sun shining for her
to see and live by, now turn dark matter
the heart moves through and pumps out,
a stream she will have to cross to reach
the present, this time to rhyme with a future
she breaks into like a thief, the house all hers,
were one's body, grief-wracked, admissible
after its faithful journey home,
its footsteps marked in an eternity of ash.

terrance hayes

—after *American Sonnets for My Past and Future Assassin*

(his voice)

I've lived inside the order
of things as they are for
so long I don't know the border
between cage and rage
except we r what we say
we r, to a point. Then the shore
fades away into a sea of
bricks. Time to scale the wall
and be done with tall tales
for good. It's a time share,
don't you know, with space
we can never leave, the line
of sight we die or live by laid on
the line as a shower of power
we step into, while mornings the sun
we shine in, darkness damns.
Only the necessity of it makes
night a story we tell.

deborah landau

--after *Soft Targets*

(her voice)

I am losing the words for
what I thought I had to say
before time runs out on us
before space walks out on us
The gun-toting men in the streets
who are they what will they
be thinking as I pass them by
as I make my way in a body
yes a soft target the news tells us
Evening and the pallor hangs
over us, will we be mourning
the end of language as we know it
the end of what we know as
what is true, will we have skin
in the game or only words.

ross gay

—after *Catalog of Unabashed Gratitude*

(his voice)

I cringe at the world's delicacy
taking me up into its arms
when I least expect it the sweat
on my brow a gushing forth from
inside the gratitude I'll feel for
the rest of my life it's why we're
here isn't it the vine trellis I'm shaped
like, rising like sap in the tree of
the world I call home in all ways
never to be lost in again without
this simmering in my blood telling
me we have places to go and nowhere
to get to other than the outermost
precincts of Otherness I hold delicately
now in my arms my thoughts my mind
taking me unabashedly to where joy is.

gabrielle calvocoressi

i

She installs the heart in the upper
tiers of heaven and lets down her
hair for a spin, hell-wise, by the
music of both battleground and
bathhouse, where broken gets
repaired and rises to fight again
some other day, as she begs
forgiveness inside a church with
no god to hear her words.

ii (her voice)

I cry tears of damage.
I wire my losses for change.
Everything smells. Let it.
We cannot escape our fate.
Poems are vessels of life
in the face of horror and strife.
I wander in and out
of the trance state,
wishing for what I don't have;
the fear of losing what I have
keeps me going back
to the power of the cock,
brutal and mesmerizing to me.
No flower child in history
—my alter-ego—can speak

volumes better than this mystery
of genderfluidity as the face
of, call it undeserving grace.
Give me my place
in the world, is all I ask—
for this, as far as I am
concerned, is the poet's task,
tenderness and peace be damned.

iii — after a poem of hers

Hardness of heart she hurt into early
was salvage of herself deep and late,
for the cycles she would soften for,
that led her into knowledge of fate.
She stood up and conquered fear
that settled into her bones, lonely
to the core she would live out of
at all cost, knowing blood moves
the truth to heal, sweet and desolate.

matthew dickman

—after a poem of his

The world-famous scientist with a debilitating illness dies,
the young hacker who turned in the whistleblower dies,
the marriage of the infamous president's eldest son lies
in tatters, and so on goes the news of the day
while he who tends the garden of memory delicately appears
in print, his childhood exposed for all the world to see
and hear, its undercurrents of violence pulling us away
to where the world, all-devouring, lives and dies
by language caught in the mouth of the fray
we're never free of, the music of the spheres
he tunes into and out of accordingly,
as the radio in his head transubstantializes
everyday appearances, his channeled soliloquies
powering over time's gaps the Emersonian way
by American griefs that tantalize
right through the walls of unabashed Being, free.

tommye blount

—after *Fantasia for the Man in Blue*

He's nailed it, the opening, as I pause
to take it in before proceeding across
a threshold of more than music, a cross
borne by one who's broken no laws
other than the color of his skin, being
Other in a neighborhood where walking
is a crime, the beat patrolled by history
on two feet, that has truck with fantasy
stirred to perfection and disabused
of what exactly, innocence suffused
with the body's loneliness? I'm confused
but keep reading, the two of us fused
as one, brothers on the printed page
eschewing a fraternal message
for the homoerotic one, one I try
to understand, am given to understand
is beyond understanding, that some people die
for lack of. He measures the stand
he takes in the fact of his body's desire,
the doggerel he raises himself above like the fire
that has him burning at both ends, for hire.

miho nonaka

—after *The Museum of Small Bones*

The ones who get heard
write of bones:
The museum of small bones;
good bones;
angel bones.
But the skin peeled
to get there
is the skeleton's
voice, who knew
all along its
own sound,
like the gurgling of the brook
behind the house
in early July.
This island country
is where I will die,
she makes me see,
reading her discrete
sentences, learning
the lay of her bifurcated mind.

Old Meiji-period film clips,
colorized, of Ginza
street theater, faces peering
out at the unseen
camera, the one
through whose eyes

we watch the scene unfold,
conveys something of
her feints and dodges,
her vanishing
between the lines
that say: Running late
but on the way!
Stay skeptical,
she adds,
of my arriving.
Like a silkworm turned
translucent, pure
from its cocoon,
a body not to be owned,
shroud-making the while.

jericho brown

i (his voice)

The default setting of my life
is strife, pure and simple,
and nothing, no poem, can
change that. But singing
can make it easier to bear,
and the color barrier easier
to live with. Which is not
to say politics is off the table
of a poem. Au contraire. We
sing for power to change hands
and don't we know it. Still,
the bird chirps and trills
in springtime in the garden
of wherever you are, before winter
shuts us down for good. Ice
in our veins. Solid block of time.
Make and unmake ourselves all we will.
River me this or that these moments
we live by, and for, banking on
remembrance to blossom anew
the heartbeat we know is ours,
that gets us to the ocean in time.

ii — after *The Tradition*

Rage read all ways but one: white
of the eyes the Black man stares

back into, to get the measure of
the cells they're both in, for all
that self-expression frees. The
wounded body he inherits is his
subject, the object being to heal
or survive the tradition he wants
no part of, is apart from, is part
of, toeing the color line of America
to its grave and back, ...a whole man.

ilya kaminsky

— after *Deaf Republic*

(his voice)

I imagined
you
were not what i
imagined, and so
you
were,
a talisman worn
on the sleeve of
justice, that i
sought fruitlessly
in the streets
of my past, where
we had gone,
where we had
a hand in making
a difference—
seen not too
late, not too
soon but all of
us holding on
as best we could
to the dream
of an engaged citizenry
eager to feel
again the weight

not of history
but of our bodies,
the source of all
our imaginings
at night
before we sleep
in each other's
arms, before we err
yet again on the side
of hearing our names
spoken in
the silence
that named us.

*

Longing for you,
not for beauty per se
but its absence
holding us
together,
your hair wrapping me
in its length
of desire
which you foretold
with a smile I'd give
anything to see
were I not deaf,
were not the sound of
your voice, your mouth
opening and closing
for a breath's sake,
our death foretold

in words
I could not hear,
or bear to.

maggie smith

—after *Good Bones*

This otherness at full tilt,
an embrace of time and
space, calls the self down
to its essentials, the way
there's a birthday for every
day, week, month of the year
to leave its fingerprints on
the covers of death, that
story we hear told, one way
or another, all our lives.

*

A perfectly shaped thought
escapes by way of
silence taking hold of it.

*

Two sagi—herons—waves rippling in air
flying overhead in the late May sky,
are heroes to me as I watch them
disappear out of sight. They cut
themselves off from the night
they are traveling to, and through,
though it's early evening here

where blue, transparent as glass,
is the true color of darkened light.

*

She wins the trust of the reader
by taking the bitter world to task
for its lies and deceit, while its mask
of wholeness as the narrative
we'd invest in, word for word,
not lost on her either, but only believed
as far as her sentence would take her,
as far as her craft would carry her.

nicole sealey

— on a poem of hers

(her voice)

the white man won't man up
the white man won't get down
the white man wants to get out
and about with his privilege
intact but history is not on his
side the white man all but owned
it once but not anymore amen

reginald dwayne betts

Prison spelled not his doom nor demise
but his dare-to-be-a-poet, it broke loose
in him the words he needed to realize
were his alone to say, without excuse,
without regret, no, with regret, a story
that owns the fact of guilt without end,
a sinner's confession that would suspend
disbelief on the wings of hourless mystery
that the world, he knows, would countermand
like 'the blackened flower,'
though the struggle to survive is his power.

katie ferris

—on some poems of hers

i (her voice)

It isn't Death's fault
I'm here basking in aftermath,
or taking a bath in melancholy,
or wishing for a different path
to take me where I've never been.
It's a bee in my bonnet I let loose
between these lines, a hive
I've got hidden under my dress.
See what you'll be missing when
—or is it after—you turn the page?
I won't tell you my age but
neither will I keep it from you. Besides,
the guessing game I like to play
makes hay with the buzzing
in my skull. Hear it?

jay deshpande

—on a poem of his

(his voice)

I died and went to heaven and had
to return somehow to the hell
of daily life but found there pleasures
I had overlooked, now fondly recalled
with contradiction as my lantern
in the night I will never name.

lana bella

—on some poems of hers

(her voice)

Here darkness purrs like a revved engine.
Here the void empties into intolerable nightmares.
Here women hang themselves by desire
only to cut the cord at the end of their breath,
showering in a mist of a profusion of senses.
We endure for their sake, the little ones
on their way behind us, as they follow
our beat one after the other into collusion.
Dream on, dreamer, the hawk's eye bids you
farewell.

ocean vuong

i

He uses the words, he hoists the phrases
history gets itself known by, careful
meanwhile of letting eternity speak its truth
between the lines, lines gushing forth in poetry
he couldn't stop if he tried, lines he lives for.

ii —after *Night Sky with Exit Wounds*

(his voice)

And I am hand
that clasps yours,
to understand arm.

And I am what
risks harm when
I enter this language
on tiny feet.

And I am brutal
in detailing the losses
incurred by the war
I never fought more
than on this page.

And I am ready
to die to be able
to say the poem
you are to me.

franny choi

— after reading a poem of hers

(her voice)

The tears that collect and pool at the bottom
of my poem will one day carry me
like a river to wider shores where
my name, like a wave, will swallow
the past and show me a way forward
into a sunlight these words foretell,
shining down upon the darkness I am
and will never betray, so help me korea.
This my oath to my foremothers and forefathers
in this poem stolen for
my name, my otherness, my home.

Epilogue

The reader's tale

Urashima visiting the kingdom undersea
lingered many a long day, in no hurry
to find his way home again, enchanted he
was by the sounds he heard that beautifully
dreamed up the world's loving cup
from which he drank abundantly, grateful to
put past him the myriad cities of the map
of home he sometimes remembered through
a word here, a word there or a sentence
overheard that held him entranced.
But years passed, until there wasn't a trace
left he could recall, a grace
that might have been amazing were it not
for the subliminal claim on him
in the waters he had learned to swim.
Today was no exception. But the knot
he untied on the box astonishingly wide
as it was deep, was the ribbon of his youth
that unraveled swiftly in air. He sighed
for all he'd lost: no clue to the truth
he'd spent all these years searching faithfully.

Tracing backwards in no order
save haphazardly chronological, he began
to wonder, who was the man whom he
arrived on these shores to become, dryly
observing wave after wave that had crashed

against now rock, now sand, every particle
of which had helped him stand his ground.
And the ironies he found were not lost
on him, the yearly ceremony of musical
chairs at no roundtable he ever sat at, trust
me, notwithstanding. The seat was sound,
it's true, wherever he sat, by which flashed
like stars shooting across the sky, sudden
insights into the question Why, if not Who,
and braving uncertainties being his forte,
it was enough for him. So sat he, who knew
the dangers of believing dreams that don't lie.
Not by any stretch of the imagination anyway.
Lightworking some called it. Not he. The die
had been cast ten thousand days prior to
whatever night fancy had brought him to sing.
Call it the changing light in Nipponland,
the one that called him in service of And.

Now his fate amazed him in its maze-
like permutations under close watch.
Americaless, geographically at least,
he put his foot down at every line he
crossed to get to wherever he was going
(out the door) to further contact with…
Grande size! …though supine on the ground
like a drone taken out of the sky…Hi ace!
though crawling down his Open Road…& so on…
What is nakedness but the aim to redress imbalance?
You don't want to sink into your own private
narrative—you must remain in the shared
public narrative, which is your era's, fated as time.
For Urashima got away with his youth intact,

the box unlooked in, until he got back home
and couldn't resist the glowing embers
buried deep inside there, all a-shine with
memories that, once restored, made
him asinine with the rest of the past
when looked at from the luminous present—
the island of remembrances his home
instead, till the end of his now white-haired days.

***

Acknowledgements

Some of these poems, several in earlier or different forms, originally appeared in the following journals:

DIOGEN: pro culture magazine Jan. 2016 (Europe): "craig arnold."

Journal of Poetics Research March 2017 (Australia): "joseph brodsky"

KIYO: Bulletin of The Society of Humanities, Kanto Gakuin University, No. 138, July 20, 2018 (Japan): "walt whitman and emily dickinson."

KIYO: Bulletin of The Society of Humanities, Kanto Gakuin University, No. 139, December 20, 2018 (Japan): "herman melville," "edgar allan poe," "edgar lee masters," "stephen crane," "robert frost," "wallace stevens," william carlos "williams," "ezra pound."

KIYO: Bulletin of The Society of Humanities, Kanto Gakuin University, No. 140, July 25, 2019 (Japan): "charles bukowski," "richard wilbur," "grace paley," "jack gilbert," "bob kaufman," "james merrill," "robert creeley," "john ashbery," "galway kinnell," "w.s. merwin," "james wright," "philip levine," "anne sexton."

KIYO: Bulletin of The Society of Humanities, Kanto Gakuin University, No. 141, December 20, 2019 (Japan): "derek walcott," "peter everwine," "sylvia plath," "mark strand," "mary oliver."

Mascara Literary Magazine Fall 2015 (Australia): "emily dickinson" (section)

Poetry Kanto 2015 No. 31 (Japan) *"edgar allen poe" (section)*

TRANSACTIONS: Humanities Research Institute, Kanto Gakuin University, No. 42, February 20, 2019 (Japan): "marianne moore," "robinson jeffers," "t.s. eliot," e.e. cummings," "hart crane," "stanley kunitz," "theodore roethke," "elizabeth bishop," "william everson," "john berryman," "robert lowell," "robert duncan."

After a decade-long labor of love as editor of *Poetry Kanto*—generously introducing countless American poets to Japanese audiences—Alan Botsford, now, in *possessions,* returns home to celebrate and pay homage to nearly two hundred American poets in all their wild diversity, clamor of voices, homing and homelessness, yawps, love letters, rebellions, and recriminations. It's a great homage to all of our American poets. A testament of American poetry since Whitman. Great, capacious poems. I know of no other book like this. *possessions* calls American poets to a festival, a jubilee, where each one stands in Botsford's verse like a leaf of grass in Whitman's poetic vision of democracy, brotherhood, sisterhood, and love.

—Michael Sowder, author of *House Under the Moon* and *Whitman's Ecstatic Union: Conversion and Ideology in Leaves of Grass*

Alan Botsford's book *possessions* explores an essential aesthetic truth: namely, that the individual poet's voice takes shape over time through the deep reading of other poets. His poems, utterly his own, engage with forebears such as Walt Whitman, Emily Dickinson, and Herman Melville; modernists, ranging from Gertrude Stein to Stephen Crane, from William Carlos Williams to T.S. Eliot; and a wide array of contemporary poets. "It is in this flow I locate, such as it is, the I," he asserts in his prologue, an assertion borne out, in kaleidoscopic and startling ways, in all of the poems that follow.

—Jennifer Barber, author of *Works on Paper*, and founding editor of *Salamander*

Alan Botsford has written an epic love song to American poetry, a song that maps a topography of the spirit, inspired by the works of poets from Whitman to Rankine. Through a persistent encounter with poems written by others, Botsford has found a large-enough form, an "island of remembrances, a home till the end of his now white haired days." As they have for Mr. Botsford, the 155 "duets" in this collection will also "press *our* human minds to hear their own singing."

—Jennifer Wallace, author of *Almost Entirely* and former editor of *The Cortland Review*

"Prodigious...Even as his dedicated responses are about the poets, a reader is listening to Botsford revealing himself & constantly asking himself what will suffice, what can I praise & take to heart, what can I level with. I don't know how he did all this. And he, alone, could span cultures the way he does. His book astounds me for its all-encompassing energy. ... I sense his book as a cosmos.... The scale of his endeavor here impresses & amazes me. All the poets who see it, who are part of his ruminations & entrances into their voices/visions will say of course more, more, but will be grateful. As I am.

—William Heyen, American poet, literary critic, editor

I was deeply moved... an ambitious and original work...There is so much to absorb, to ruminate on and to entertain the questions the work raises...Possessions is a wonderful title—a wonderful concept for this collection. It is a very ambitious work—and seems quite original to me. It would be wonderful teaching tool in the classroom. I could imagine spending a whole semester with it, the poems themselves and using them as a springboard for students to examine their own reactions and ideas— being immersed in this "magnitude of vision." The language and imagery are often arresting —("music made for angels"—and on and on.) Your understanding of the poets of affliction here, Lowell, for example, resonates deeply. I am touched by the heart of these poems and by the "white heat" of them. I could get lost in the connections, interconnections of it, part of the power of this work....this work requires much time given its depth and expansiveness and what it so powerfully engenders in the reader.

—Adele Ne Jame, author of *Field Work* and *The South Wind*

...the idea of writing a sort of epic love letter in verse to American poetry and poets is a great one. Many of the individual poems are really strong engagements with individual poets. Ones that stood out for me .... are the ones to James Tate (a perfect lyric), Anis Shivani, Yusef Komunyakaa, Herman Melville, Mark Strand, Harold Bloom, Marie Howe, Joseph Brodsky, C.K. Williams, Jorie Graham, Louise Glück and Charles Bernstein.

—Michael S. Collins, author of *The Travelling Queen* and *Understanding Etheridge Knight*

...a lovely, spirited, engaging, and erudite read...unique in its design, though clearly informed with / by/ in the tradition(s) of American and British poetry...I feel the language moves / alive on the page and it informs, and all of this so seemingly effortlessly...A most ambitious work. Epic and generous.

—Gregory Dunne, author of *Quiet Accomplishment: Remembering Cid Corman*, poetry editor of *Kyoto Journal*

This book boldly sets out to capture the voices and spirits of many of the most fascinating figures in contemporary English and Japanese poetry. Forging these kinds of connections over time and space provide sustenance for the soul, and as readers, we follow Botsford across the divides of time and space, identifying across eras, ethnicity, and nationality.

—Jeffrey Angles, award-winning American and Japanese poet and translator

It is certainly a very impressive book in so many ways. First, the scope of the book is majestic. It's sort of like a poetic companion to the Norton Anthology of Modern Poetry, with an expanded list of poets. …it's obvious that he has a real mastery of the literature and is able to expand on it. …Some of the poems are in his own voice and others in the voice of the poet and still others in a third-person voice writing about the poets from a sort of detached perspective (like a scholarly evaluation written in verse?). …With "possessions" I think he gets credit for creating an entirely new genre! …the poetry holds up entirely on its own without the reader really needing to know anything about the poets themselves. Knowing more definitely helps, of course, but isn't absolutely necessary. In addition, I'm sure that the book will introduce readers to many poets they might not become acquainted with otherwise. …All in all, I found the book to be both enjoyable and impressive! It deserves a wide audience."

—Richard Evanoff, author of *Bioregionalism and Global Ethics: A Transactional Approach to Achieving Ecological Sustainability, Social Justice, and Human Well-being*